THE RURAL CHURCH

Creative Leadership Series

The Rural Church: Learning from Three Decades of Change

Edward W. Hassinger,
John S. Holik, and
J. Kenneth Benson

Creative Leadership Series
Lyle E. Schaller, Editor

Abingdon Press / Nashville

The Rural Church: Learning from Three Decades of Change

Copyright © 1988 by Abingdon Press

This book is printed on acid-free paper.

Library of Congress Cataloging-in-Publication Data

HASSINGER, EDWARD WESLEY.
  The rural church.
  (Creative leadership series)
  Bibliography: p.
  1. Rural churches—United States. I. Holik, John S., 1924–
  II. Benson, J. Kenneth.
  III. Title. IV. Series.
  BV638.H33   1988   250'.9173'4   87-33691

ISBN 0-687-36587-2

MANUFACTURED BY THE PARTHENON PRESS AT
NASHVILLE, TENNESSEE, UNITED STATES OF AMERICA

Foreword

How should we respond to the rural crisis?
The 1980s placed that question in the campaign
speech of every candidate for the presidency of
the United States, on the agenda of thousands of
local rural church leaders, and on the list of
urgent concerns for the annual meetings of
dozens of Protestant denominations.

As the number of farmers filing for bankruptcy
quadrupled in the space of four years and farms
that had been held in the same families for three
or four generations were sold to pay off huge
bank loans, the television networks made the
crisis national news. The economic squeeze
experienced by farmers was passed on to
farm-implement dealers, hardware store owners, grocers, druggists, and other small-town
retailers. And when the aged physicians who
had served some of those small towns for a half
century reluctantly retired, no replacements
appeared on the scene.

Pressures back in the 1940s to consolidate the

public schools had replaced the little white schoolhouse with the yellow school bus. When the local high school was closed following construction of the huge consolidated school, often located five miles outside any municipality, a cohesive force in community life disappeared. In many cases that old brick school building was converted into the local senior citizens' center. The crowds that once came to watch teenagers play basketball did not reassemble to watch mature adults crochet or play checkers.

The mid- and late 1980s also brought the closing of scores of small hospitals. The usual result was a trip of thirty to one hundred miles or more to a larger hospital.

The number of farms that ranged between 100 and 179 acres—the traditional family farm—dropped from 1,438,000 in 1935 to 773,000 in 1959, to fewer than 350,000 in 1986. The average size of the U.S. farm climbed from 195 acres in 1935 to 460 acres in 1985. Larger farms meant fewer farmers; the number of people living on farms dropped from 30.2 million in 1940 to 23 million in 1950, to 15.6 million in 1960, to 9.7 million in 1970, to 7.2 million in 1980, to approximately 5 million in 1986.

Fewer farmers meant fewer customers for the merchants in town and fewer members for the rural churches.

This decline in the farm population was partially offset, however, by the movement of citizens of all ages to rural areas. Some came to retire; many more came to enjoy the peace and quiet of rural life, while commuting an hour or more each way to a city paycheck. A great many urban parents, alarmed by urban crime, the availability of drugs, the depersonalization of the huge urban schools, and the increase in the number of unmarried teenage mothers, decided the country atmosphere was superior to city life as an environment for their children. Back in 1940 the rural population peaked at 57.2 million and began to decline. By 1970 it was down to 53.9 million, but then rural living began to exert a strong attraction. By the mid-1980s the rural population of the U. S. exceeded 60 million, and each year since has brought a new record high.

Perhaps the biggest but largely ignored change is that retirees are replacing farmers in the rural U.S. In scores of rural counties the number of couples receiving Social Security benefits exceeds the number of full-time farm families by a two-to-one ratio. The U.S. Postal Service, which delivers the Social Security, pension, and dividend checks, often contributes more to the net personal income of the residents than does agriculture or manufacturing or retail trade or the local school system. In a couple of hundred rural counties, residents age 65 and over account for one-fifth to one-third of the total population. Since persons past age 60 are almost twice as likely to be in church on the average Sunday morning as those age 18 to 24, the graying of the rural nation cannot be described as a threat to the rural church. It also should be added that since the average annual cash contributions to religious causes by people age 65 and over greatly exceed the average for those age 25 to 54, the graying of rural people will undergird, not undercut the financial base of the rural church.

The graying of our rural areas is reflected in the fact that in one-fifth of the congregations covered by this survey, at least half the members had already celebrated their sixty-fifth birthday. The shift to a nonagricultural economy is reflected by the fact that only one-fourth of the congregations were described as "farmers' churches."

The changing nature of the rural U.S. raises three important questions for church leaders, both congregational and denominational. The first, perhaps at the top of most people's agenda, concerns the health and vitality of the rural church. This book by Professor Edward W. Hassinger and his colleagues makes it clear that the answer is favorable. Their research indicates that rural churches are both tough and healthy.

In answer to the second question, What has happened during these past three decades that have brought these unprecedented changes? these three researchers offer a remarkable response. The churches in ninety-nine rural townships were studied in 1952, restudied in 1967, and the whole process replicated in 1982. This is a unique study without parallel in either urban or rural areas and offers scores of insights into the nature, life, and ministry of the rural church.

The third question is directed at the leaders who formulate the policies that affect rural America. What is happening in rural America that should influence denominational and congregational policies? What are the issues and concerns we should be addressing?

For those convinced that financial subsidies will be required to enable rural congregations to continue to keep their doors open, the first question may be, Where will the funds come from for these subsidies? This study reveals the best answer—Don't worry. Only eight of the 492 reporting congregations in this survey received any direct financial assistance from their denominations! While the demand for financial subsidies may increase as more middle- and upper-middle-class people move to rural areas (their expectations in regard to subsidies and their skill in soliciting them greatly exceeds those of lower- and lower-middle-class citizens), the real need probably will decrease as rural churches become increasingly oriented toward mature adults.

The vital rural church, like the efficient and productive family farmer, does not see a need for huge financial subsidies. The leaders of these churches usually recognize that direct financial subsidies can be addictive, may undermine the economic health of the congregations, often create an adversary relationship between the source of the subsidy and the recipient, frequently result in a sense of dependency, and may inhibit initiative.

Indirect subsidies often are more acceptable. In several states, for example, farm land is assessed, for general property taxes, at a lower percentage of market value than the ratio applied to all other real estate. Likewise, the regional judicatories of several denominations have developed a formula for calculating askings and apportionments that benefits small congregations and penalizes large churches.

In general, however, there is no reason to expect that denominational subsidies will be required to maintain Protestant churches in our rural areas.

The only area in which the demand for subsidies may increase will be in those denominations concerned about the employment of clergy. The demand to subsidize the salaries of full-time but underemployed clergy may increase in the years ahead.

The good news is that our rural areas provide a fertile setting for the bivocational pastor. This already has been recognized and affirmed by thousands of Southern Baptist, Presbyterian, Episcopal, and Church of the Nazarene ministers. Nearly one-half (45%) of the ministers in this survey held secular jobs, and three out of five of these bivocational clergy had full-time secular employment. About half of these pastors with full-time secular employment held white-collar jobs. The economic viability of many rural churches is dependent upon the concept of the bivocational minister.

Those who worry about the future supply of pastors for rural churches will find grounds for continued apprehension from the data in this report. Today approximately one-fourth of all our people live in rural communities, and that number includes a disproportionately large number of mature adults.

This survey revealed that in 1982, 65 percent of all ministers questioned grew up in a rural area, down from 78 percent thirty years earlier. Where will their successors come from in the decades ahead? Part of the answer may come from among adults reared in urban areas who, as they approach retirement, see the pastoral ministry as a second career. Who will enlist those people for a new vocation—the congregation? denominational leaders? the seminaries?

An overlapping issue concerns educational requirements for the pastoral ministry. A growing number of denominations require a seminary degree for full ordination. Will mature adults seeking a new calling be willing to meet that requirement?

What if they do? The popular stereotype of the past hundred years is that seminarians are substantially more liberal in theology, biblical interpretation, and similar questions upon graduation than when they entered seminary. If that is true, how will it affect the supply of pastors for rural churches? When asked about their theological position in 1967, two-thirds of those rural ministers identified themselves as either "conservative" or "fundamentalist." Fifteen years later, that proportion had climbed to 85 percent. The cry in the 1960s was that theological seminaries should be "urban, ecumenical and university related." The evidence of the past quarter-century suggests that such an approach to theological education may not produce the best urban pastors. It is unlikely to produce the next generation of happy and effective pastors for rural churches. The distinction the authors draw in this book between "Preacher Bob" and "the Reverend Jones" is one that should be studied by everyone responsible for the next generation of ministers for the rural U.S.

Another policy issue for church leaders is the distinction between "small" and "rural." In several denominations, policy makers often link these two words together. This book makes clear that while many rural churches have relatively few members, others are large and growing.

The greatest correlation is not between "small" and "rural" or "large" and "urban," but between denominational culture and size. For the nation as a whole, for example, only 7 percent of all Lutheran Church-Missouri Synod and 8 percent of all Evangelical Lutheran Church in America congregations average fewer than 35 people at worship. By contrast, 27 percent of all United Methodist congregations average fewer than 35 at worship. This suggests that the size of congregations is at least as much a function of the denominational culture as of the geographical setting. This also suggests that the role of the bivocational pastor should be placed higher on the agenda of United Methodist policy makers than on Lutheran agendas.

One of the most significant changes lifted up in this research is the decline in the number of congregations that meet in buildings located in the open country and the sharp increase in the number of churches in large villages. One facet of this of interest to denominational policy makers is the decline in the number of churches in the open country, where the mainline Protestant denominations historically have been strongest. The increase in the number of churches in the larger villages came largely from nonmainline sources. Should denominational leaders urge open-country churches to close? Or relocate to a large village? The historical record strongly suggests that encouraging open-country congregations to merge with churches in town is not a productive road toward church growth. The obvious four choices for many denominations appear to be: (a) encourage open-country congregations to relocate to town; (b) organize new congregations in town; (c) cut back in the number of congregations and number of members; or (d) encourage existing congregations to change so as to accommodate more people. Experience suggests the third alternative is the easiest to implement and the fourth is the most difficult.

For some readers, a critical concern is that

every congregation should be involved in the life of the larger community. Those espousing this point of view will be delighted to read of the sharp increase in community involvement of the churches in this survey. In 1967 only 24 percent of all churches supported one or more community programs such as youth organizations, civil rights organizations, antipoverty programs, and temperance efforts. Fifteen years later, that proportion had climbed to 42 percent, with 48 percent of the mainline churches supporting one or more community programs. As could be expected, the larger the congregation, the more likely that church would be supporting community programs.

Those who favor intercongregational cooperation also will be pleased to note that the proportion of congregations engaging in this expression of cooperation increased from 46 percent in 1967 to 53 percent in 1982.

How can denominational leaders and agencies assist the small rural church? For many, that is the most pressing question. One response could be to help in expanding the organizational life of small rural churches. At the top of that list would be assistance in strengthening and expanding the Sunday school. Thirteen out of fourteen of the churches covered in the survey maintained a Sunday school, while fewer than half had a choir, only one-sixth had a men's organization and 10 percent offered a young-adult group.

Strengthening the organizational life of the small church, both rural and urban, could be a productive means of enabling these congregations to reach, serve, and assimilate more people.

Two other issues of interest to those responsible for ministerial placement merit mention here. The first, and perhaps least surprising, is that the smaller the congregation, the more likely the minister is to stand at the extremely conservative end of the theological spectrum. The larger the congregation, the more likely it is that the pastor is closer to the liberal end of the spectrum. This fact of life has been rediscovered repeatedly by those who have encouraged the small congregation meeting in a building in the open country to merge with a large church in town. The basic point, however, is that ministers in rural churches should not be perceived as identical and interchangeable parts.

The other half of this picture reflects the professionalization of the parish ministry. In 1952 fewer than 12 percent of the congregations in this survey provided an office for the pastor. By 1967 that proportion had doubled to 23 percent, and in 1982, 42 percent of all congregations provided such an office.

When the question of providing a parsonage was raised in 1952, only 54 percent of the churches with 100 or more members provided houses for the ministers. That proportion peaked at 66 percent in 1967 and was down to 60 percent in 1982.

Of equal interest is the fact that in 1982, two-thirds of all congregations reported a

15

kitchen in the church building, up from only one-fourth in 1952.

The acceptable level of facilities had climbed substantially in thirty years, and that can become a significant issue when the minister born in 1925 retires and is to be replaced by one born after the end of World War II. Each succeeding generation has higher expectations.

For those interested in the increasing number of women going to theological seminaries, the big shock in this report may be that in 1952 (see chapter 6) 97 percent of the ministers serving this group of rural churches was male. Thirty years later that proportion was still 97 percent. What happened? Why had that figure not dropped to 91 or 92 percent, or lower?

Perhaps it was because, when compared to the geographical distribution of churches, a disproportionately large number of women going into the parish ministry came from urban backgrounds? Perhaps it was a result of the more conservative stance of rural churches? Perhaps it was because a disproportionately large number of women going into the parish ministry serve on the staff of large congregations? Perhaps this lack of change in that percentage is a result of the large proportion of these congregations with bivocational ministers? Or could the lack of employment opportunities for the lay husband of the ordained woman be a significant factor? Or can this be explained by the preferences of women graduating from seminary? Or is the primary reason the opposition to the ordination of women by several denominations heavily represented in these rural townships? Or is the number-one reason the decline in the number of congregations among those denominations that do ordain women?

Perhaps in the year 1997 or 2002, someone will make a fourth visit and discover the proportion of males serving these rural churches will have dropped significantly.

Whatever the factors behind this lack of change, these figures highlight another policy question for the agenda of those denominations that do ordain women.

Finally, and for some policy makers this may be of the greatest interest, this study documents the numerical decline of the mainline denominations and the rise of other churches since the end of the Second World War.

The original survey in 1952 counted a total of 547 churches in these 99 rural townships. Most—400 to be exact—were affiliated with one of the mainline denominations. Between 1952 and 1982 the total number of congregations dropped by 32, to 515. The mainline denominations added 28 and lost 83, for a net decrease of 55 congregations. By contrast, the nonmainline churches reported a gain of 70 and a loss of 47, for a net gain of 23 congregations.

These figures may help to explain why, when asked their perception of what the next ten years will bring, more than three-quarters of the nonmainline congregations expected to grow in size. By contrast, only 55 percent of the churches affiliated with the mainline denominations expected they would be larger ten years hence.

For those churches with fewer than 50 members, nearly three-quarters of the nonmainline congregations expected the next years would bring growth, and only 4.4 percent expected their churches would close. In the mainline churches, only 38 percent believed the future would bring growth, and 18.5 percent expected their churches would be closed within ten years.

Is that difference a product of denominational affiliation? Or a result of the length of time a congregation has been in existence? The answer to that question could create a self-fulfilling prophecy.

These are only a few of the questions raised by this landmark study on the changing nature of our rural church, and its characteristics, ministry, and outreach. The reader will find here a revealing and provocative introduction to many other changes.

Lyle E. Schaller
Yokefellow Institute
Richmond, Indiana

Contents

Acknowledgments

The research on which this report is based has a long history. The original survey was directed by Lawrence M. Hepple; field work began in 1952 with support from the Rockefeller Foundation. The 1967 study was conducted by the authors of the present report, with financial support from the Interagency Committee on Research of The Methodist Church, The Board of National Missions of the United Presbyterian Church in the U.S.A., and the Christian Church (Disciples of Christ) in Missouri. The latest survey, in 1982, was supported by a grant from the Lilly Endowment, Inc. In all the research episodes, the Missouri Agricultural Experiment Station has been a contributor.

We express our debt to Charles Moore, who participated in the early stages of the most recent survey; to the interviewers for their careful attention to details; to Bernadette Kulas for field work oversight and data processing; to Isabelle C. Hassinger for her work on the manuscript, which went far beyond routine editing; and to Deborah Garrett for skillful manuscript preparation. Our deep appreciation is extended to Dr. Robert W. Lynn, Vice President for Religion of

ACKNOWLEDGMENTS

Lilly Endowment, Inc., for his interest in and support of the project; and to Dr. Lyle E. Schaller for seeing the manuscript through to publication and for the Foreword, in which he draws implications from the study for policy makers and practitioners. More than most, that Foreword is an integral part of the report, serving also as its epilogue. Finally, we thank the ministers and other people in the local communities who helped us with the study.

Edward W. Hassinger
John S. Holik
J. Kenneth Benson

I

The Rural Church
in Perspective

The Keytesville Presbyterian Church, a tidy white building in a rural Missouri setting, looks like a picture postcard. We stop to learn more about this picturesque church; surely it provides a clue to the status of churches in rural communities. We are surprised, however; the building no longer houses an active congregation but is preserved as a museum piece, listed on the National Register of Historic Places. It's like the one-room school a local insurance company maintains on its grounds as a nostalgic reminder of an institution that truly has passed from the rural scene. Is this to be the fate of the rural church?

Fear of the demise of the rural church is a familiar theme. So, how fares that church? In terms of survival, it has fared quite well. Results from our detailed study of churches in the rural heartland of the U.S. showed only a slight loss in number of congregations over a thirty-year period. Some changes not so easily detected—changes in facilities, organization, and leadership (clergy)—will be described in the context of a changing rural society.

Without question, our rural society has changed greatly in this century, with important implications for rural churches. The farm population has plummeted from 30 percent of the nation's total in 1920 to 2 percent at the present time. Agriculture has become a minority occupation in the rural U.S. Isolation has been broken by modern transportation and communication. Electricity has lighted and powered homes. Social class divisions have become more pronounced in a more diverse population. And, patterns of institutional organizations have been transformed.

Changes in institutional organizations are especially pertinent to the discussion of the rural church. In general, these organizations have changed their emphasis from informal relationships to formal relationships. They have been consolidated, thereby becoming larger and fewer, and have become more interdependent with the bureaucracies of the larger society. While no single term does justice in describing these changes, we use the term "urbanization of rural society" to summarize them. The rural school is a good example of an institutional organization that has followed this route of change. From a small neighborhood institution, it has moved through consolidation to a larger area-wide facility dependent on the state for resources, and yielding to the state a substantial measure of control.

Has the rural church followed a parallel route? It has not. Let's amend that by saying the rural church has not reacted to the urbanization of rural society to the extent that the school and selected other institutional organizations have. The research reported in this book not only arrives at that conclusion, but seeks to discover why the rural church departs from that pattern.

In order to introduce the reader to rural churches in Missouri, we will conduct a "windshield survey" of the state, followed by a discussion of the historic and social contexts of the rural churches. And we will describe the way this research was conducted.

A Windshield Survey of Rural Churches. We begin our windshield survey by leaving the interstate highways of Missouri and driving leisurely through the countryside. We encounter numerous small towns and many churches located in the open country. If churches are not directly observed, roadside signs may indicate their direction and distance. At the edge of many towns, a sign offers a welcome from the churches in the community, but the listing usually is not a complete directory of the local religious groups. Most likely to be missing are groups such as Pentecostal and Holiness congregations. On close inspection, some regularities emerge. Denominational names are repeated—Baptist, Methodist, Christian (Disciples of Christ), Churches of Christ, Assemblies of God. But it is somewhat unusual to come across an Episcopal church and, if a Roman Catholic or Lutheran church is encountered, it is surmised that you are in an ethnic area. This is often confirmed by architectural features of nearby homes, or at least by names on mailboxes.

Although religious leaders often declare that the local church is not a physical facility but a body of believers, its building, grounds, and location in the community display the congregation's presence and convey a message about it. Outward appearances at least hint at, and sometimes proclaim, a congregation's age, size, affluence, and its devotion to simplicity or ostentation. Symbols—crosses, spires, red doors, white pillars, neon signs—tend to identify congregations of different traditions. And congregations name themselves—names which appear on the buildings or on signboards—often with the founding date, many before the turn of the century. In most cases the names are as unpretentious as the buildings themselves. Most churches simply take the name of their neighborhood or village (or the neighborhood or village takes the name of the church)—Hazel Creek Primitive Baptist, Mount Pleasant United Methodist, Round Prairie Baptist, Lilbourn Apostolic Church of Jesus Christ, Ironton Assembly of God, Martinsburg Community Church. Other congregations take names of religious significance—Antioch Christian, Bethlehem Baptist, Mt. Zion Christian, St. Ann's Catholic, Asbury Methodist, Knox Presbyterian, St. James A.M.E., St. Paul's Lutheran. Names may be direct references to divinity—Trinity United Methodist, Immanuel United Church of

Christ, Good Shepherd Church, Bread of Life Tabernacle. And they may be expressions of desired status—for example, Fellowship, Victory, New Hope—all names of Baptist churches. Some congregations declare themselves the "first" church, as in First United Methodist, even when a "second" church is not present in the community. The "given" name of a congregation usually precedes a denominational surname, but some congregations are without denominational affiliation.

There is some confusion in denominational names as they appear in local congregations. Churches of Christ and the Christian Church (Disciples of Christ), both common in rural Missouri, and of common ancestry, are different groups. Further name complications exist with Independent Christian Churches and the United Church of Christ (the latter formed from merging Congregational Christian and Evangelical and Reformed). There are also fine distinctions among churches bearing the names Church of God and Pentecostal.

As we continue our journey through rural Missouri, we see differences in the size and condition of church buildings. On occasion, a virtual cathedral in the field or on the Missouri River bluffs is observed. The buildings, however, are more likely to be modest structures sometimes in need of a coat of paint. A house trailer used as a church catches our eye, but we saw only one; perhaps there are more. Many open-country churches and some town churches have adjoining cemeteries. If a cemetery is present, it usually dates from the birth of the congregation. It is interesting to check the headstones; family names can be traced from an earlier time to the present through these marble (or granite) documents. In many cases, such tracing is easy because family plots are well maintained.

Denominational identity and outward appearance are somehow, although imperfectly, related. One comes to expect Methodist churches to have an unpretentious but well-established look—the appearance of having been there for a long time. In the villages, the Methodist church is likely to have a prominent location near the town's center. In the open country, a sign may indicate that the congregation was established before the Civil War. We are not as apt to see Presbyterian churches; when we do, they are more likely to be in the larger rural towns.

The Christian Church (Disciples of Christ) tends to resemble the Methodist or Presbyterian in physical appearance and location in the community, but the Churches of Christ facilities are more varied in appearance. Even casual observation can detect substantial differences among Churches of Christ buildings. They range from the very modest to substantial structures. And there are sectional differences: In the southern part of the state (especially the Bootheel), Churches of Christ are more likely to have the established appearance of Methodist, Baptist, and Disciples of Christ congregations, while in the northern part, they appear more recently established and in makeshift quarters.

The denominational name most likely to be seen on church buildings or signboards is Baptist. Baptist churches are also hardest to pigeonhole in terms of outward appearance. They range from what looks like the most affluent church in town to very modest structures. Nor is it easy to classify Baptist churches by age; on the basis of signs and cornerstones, and from appearance and surroundings, we surmise that many are as old as the neighborhood or community itself. In the open country, the Baptist church may be identified with a neighborhood name and be its principal institutional prop. But other Baptist churches are newly constructed. We soon become aware of different denominational designations—Freewill, Primitive, General, Missionary, Landmark, Independent. Most often, however, the churches in Missouri are Southern Baptist. Sometimes these churches can be identifed by their white pillars, but this identifying mark is usually found only on newer and larger churches.

Not many Catholic churches appear on our drive through rural Missouri. It depends a great deal on location in the state. In the deep Ozarks, a Catholic church is likely to be found only in the larger villages, and even there it may have the appearance of an outpost church. On the other hand, in the east-central-Missouri German ethnic area that extends roughly along the Missouri River, or in the area of early French settlement that extends down the Mississippi from St. Louis, the Catholic church might be an imposing brick structure which visually dominates the small town or open country. At the same time, we notice that often there is no other church in these communities, or if there is, it is likely to be nondenominational or one of the new nonmainline denominations. In this same area, however, we also see imposing church buildings that are Lutheran (Missouri Synod) or United Church of Christ (Evangelical and Reformed), which reflect not only the religious divisions among Germans who immigrated to this area, but also their common attention to religion.

Especially in the larger villages, less often in the smaller villages and the open country, we see other churches identified as Pentecostal, Assemblies of God, or perhaps a Kingdom Hall of the Jehovah's Witnesses. These may be new structures or buildings converted from other uses. Some are continuously undergoing renovation—not on a grand scale, but piecemeal and as time and resources permit. At certain times of the year, it is common to see a banner draped across the front of the building, giving the dates of a revival.

In larger rural villages, several congregations are likely to be present. Strangers looking for mainline churches should go one block off main street (or the square); there they should expect to find substantial church buildings, either frame or brick—such is the religious-group ecology of these villages. The excursion, however, usually will not account for all the congregations in a larger village. Services might be held in a store-front among the businesses of the town, but this congregation probably would not qualify as a mainline church. Other nonmainline churches might be found nestled among residences in buildings that have been converted from a home to a church. And both mainline and nonmainline churches may offer members a new facility on the outskirts of town, built to satisfy the modern needs for parking and recreational meeting space. Most new church construction is confined to the environs of larger villages, especially those participating in the growth from "return rural migration," much more prevalent in the Ozarks than in northern or southeastern Missouri. In the small villages and open country, little new construction is apparent; older church buildings may be abandoned or have new occupants, either religious or secular.

From our windshield observations, we also gain some impression of activities associated with the churches. Activity is greatest on Sunday mornings in a two-hour span before noon. There is a break in activity between the first and second hour, representing the division between Sunday school (variously named) and worship service, but usually the same people attend both. Beginning times for Sunday services vary among congregations, but few services extend beyond noon. If we could continue our visit over the weeks of a month, we would observe that in some churches, the morning worship service is not conducted every Sunday; a regularity, usually based on every second Sunday or every fourth Sunday of the month, is maintained. On the other hand, Sunday school is probably held each week without interruption. On Sunday evenings, some of the buildings are lighted again. Attendance at these services, as viewed by comings and goings, is not as large as that at morning services. During the week, there appears to be little activity; on Wednesday evenings, and occasionally at other times, there are gatherings in some churches.

If we observed during the right week in summer, we might see use of the building in the morning for a vacation Bible school; at other times in the year, the church and grounds might be used for homecomings, bazaars, and fellowship dinners. An event of great importance in some churches is the revival, most often held on consecutive nights for a week some time during the year.

This overview orients us to the diversity of rural congregations in Missouri. In order to understand current conditions, we will continue our general assessment by placing them within a historical context and a social setting.

The Historical Context. Characteristics of the present religious landscape are greatly influenced by the frontier experience. The bold arch on the riverfront at St. Louis is a reminder of the state's historic role as the gateway in the settlement of the West. The Missouri frontier of the early 1800s was settled mostly by southern migrants, typically moving in one or two generations from Virginia through Kentucky and Tennessee. Migrants from the South in the early 1800s included many slaves; many rural blacks are their descendants.

By the middle of the century, migration was also heavy from more northern states—Illinois, Ohio, Pennsylvania, New York. This, and a sizable German immigration diluted the pro-slavery stand of the southern migrants. During the Civil War, Missouri was divided over the slavery issue, but remained in the Union. The most identifiable ethnic group in rural Missouri is German. German settlers had come to Missouri by 1820, but major immigration occurred later (Shoemaker, 1943:37). In 1839, they established a German-Lutheran colony northwest of St. Louis at Perry, from which grew the Missouri Synod Lutheran Church. In 1848, political upheaval in Germany triggered a wave of emigration, and St. Louis was a principal destination. German settlement in rural Missouri extended southward from St. Louis along the Mississippi and westward along the Missouri River (Shoemaker, 1943:39). German settlers brought their religious traditions with them—Catholic, Lutheran, and Evangelical. In 1957, the last, identified by the denomination Evangelical and Reformed, united with the Congregational Christian Church to form the United Church of Christ.

The early 1800s was a period of renewed

religious activity. Centered on the western frontier, which was just reaching Missouri, the movement is known as the Second Awakening—the Great Awakening (the first awakening) had occurred in the middle and northern colonies in the 1700s.

The main participants in the frontier revival were Baptists, Methodists, and Disciples of Christ. In common, they appealed to the frontier settlers and provided a religious form compatible with a frontier environment. In particular, they presented a salvation religion of simple organizational structure and depended heavily upon laypeople to evangelize the population. Bedell and associates (1975:156) say of Baptists, "Their lack of any centralized denominational organization and their willingness to allow itinerant and relatively unlearned ministers to evangelize the frontier areas made them prime candidates both to lead and to benefit from the new outbreaks of revival interest." Methodists also prospered on the frontier. Although that denomination was more highly structured, it benefited from use of lay preachers and traveling ministers. Peter Cartwright was a typical Methodist traveling evangelist, "a rough-hewn frontier preacher who claimed to have baptized some twelve thousand persons and to have preached over fourteen thousand sermons during his ministry in Kentucky and southern Illinois" (Bedell et al., 1975:157).

The Presbyterian Church was not particularly successful on the frontier, but two Presbyterian ministers, Barton Stone and Alexander Campbell, led separate movements which combined in 1832 to become a new denomination with a congregational organization similar to that of the Baptists. "The new denomination became known as the Disciples of Christ, or simply as 'Christians.' In the next few decades, it enjoyed phenomenal growth in the frontier areas, and the Disciples became the third major U.S. frontier religious group, along with the Baptists and Methodists" (Bedell et al., 1975:161).

Most congregations in rural Missouri today belong to those three denominations. In addition, many of the nonmainline congregations appear to be direct descendants of the frontier religious groups in style and substance. Indeed, they often proclaim that theirs is a return to "old time" religion.

Congregational governance and lay participation are a legacy of the frontier, and that influence may extend to more structural denominations. Wilhelm Pauck (1963) observed, "All American Protestant churches are in a very practical way congregationalist. Super or transcongregational authorities, church presidents or bishops or synods, cannot shape the life of local congregations except by securing the voluntary cooperation of these local groups for their plans and purposes."

The Social Context. The three distinct rural social areas of the state are the Commercial Agricultural Area, the Ozarks, and the Missouri

35

Bootheel. The Commercial Agricultural Area, north of the Missouri River and extending down the western side of the state, is typical of the Midwest in settlement patterns and farming operations. The Ozarks area has a marginal agriculture, and farmers there have long depended on off-farm employment. That section is not the "hillbilly" country of legend. The scenic area has attracted retirees and major tourist developments, and it shows a level of population growth not present in other rural areas of the state. The Missouri Bootheel, the southeast corner of the state, is rich river-bottom land where cotton, corn, wheat, and soybeans are the main cash crops; closer to Memphis, Tennessee, than to St. Louis, it is the section of the state with the largest rural black population. In all these areas, part-time farming has become more common in recent years, with off-farm employment more important as a source of family income.

An observer of long-time trends is struck with the amount of migration from the rural areas of the state. Almost all the counties in the northern and western Commercial Agricultural Area had fewer people in 1980 than in 1900; the exceptions are those counties that contain a city of some size. The losses can be attributed to the farm population; statewide, that population decreased from more than 800,000 to less than 300,000 between 1950 and 1980. However, in recent years (particularly in the 1970–1980 decade for which there is census data), the rural

Table 1.1

POPULATION OF MISSOURI BY RESIDENCE
1950–1980

Residence	Population			
	1950	1960	1970	1980
Urban	2,432,715	2,876,557	3,277,662	3,347,469
Rural	1,521,938	1,433,256	1,398,839	1,569,217
Rural Nonfarm	678,716	902,458	987,806	1,287,143
Rural Farm	843,222	540,798	411,033	282,074

Table 1.2

CHARACTERISTICS OF THE LABOR FORCE
IN RURAL MISSOURI, 1950 AND 1980

Characteristics of Labor Force in Rural Missouri	Percentages	
	1950	1980
Agricultural Workers	48.8	12.4
White-collar Workers	21.2	36.7
Blue-collar Workers	30.0	50.9
Females in Labor Force	17.9	38.7
Population over 65 Years of Age	11.5	13.8

population of Missouri has shown an increase (Table 1.1), part of a national trend referred to as the "urban-rural population turnaround."

We should hasten to note several qualifications about this trend. First, the rural farm population continues to decrease; it is in the rural *non*farm population that increases have occurred. Also of interest is that increases in the rural nonfarm population have been greater in the open country than in towns and villages. Second, not all counties share in the population increase—those concentrated in the northern Commercial Agricultural Area and some in the Bootheel do not. On the other hand, all Ozark counties have shown growth between 1970 and 1980; for some, that growth has been quite substantial. Finally, the urban-rural population turnaround appears to be temporary, and the 1990 census is likely to show a reversal of the trend.

Major changes took place in the rural labor force from 1950 to 1980 (Table 1.2). In rural Missouri, the proportion of workers engaged in agriculture declined dramatically from 49 percent to 12 percent; the proportion of women in the labor force rose from 18 percent to 39 percent; and there was an increase from 12 to14 percent in the population 65 years of age and over, the usual retirement age. The result of these changes is a more diverse labor force. Immigration of people in some rural areas and shifts in occupation suggest greater diversity in background and experience of people currently living in rural Missouri.

In our assessment of social trends, we also need to place what is happening to religious groups in the context of what is happening to contemporary rural neighborhoods and villages. In neighborhoods where once one-room schools, country stores, and churches were focal points of open-country neighborhoods consisting of farm families, now only churches are observed with any frequency. But also, the farm homes have thinned out, and we wonder if the churches established long ago remain centers of open-country neighborhoods.

There are also visible signs of change in the small towns that dot the countryside. The changes are not always what a local boosters' club would acclaim—empty school buildings, boarded-up grocery stores, closed gasoline stations. Because of better roads and nearly universal possession of automobiles, people are able to travel farther for services; at the same time, they are encouraged to do so by advertising, through both local and mass media. As a consequence, many trade centers have lost or reduced their commercial functions. By the same transportation technology, it is feasible to transport youths to consolidated schools and sick people to central health facilities. These shifts in services do not necessarily mean that a town or village dies. Many small towns almost devoid of retail, educational, or health services still maintain a residential population of people who commute to work in other places or are retired.

In a major reordering of trade centers, some towns have declined as service centers, others have become more important. The latter have been able to attract supermarket-type grocery stores, discount establishments, hardware stores, and fast-food restaurants. In such places, one might expect to find a consolidated secondary school and a community hospital. These centers draw clients from a wide rural area and become dominant commercial centers for an expanded trade area. Such centers, however, would probably exceed 2,500 population, the criterion of "rural" we are using, and thus would not be included in this study.

The decline in agricultural employment, greater diversity and reduction in isolation of the population, and consolidation of services in fewer locations are reflections of the "urbanization of rural society" described earlier. It confirms that changes in rural Missouri are not unique and suggests that the Missouri case has wide application for other rural churches.

Naturally, churches respond to demographic and ecological change. Congregations may be established in growing communities and closed in contracting communities. Churches, though, seem to have been less affected by these changes of rural society than have other social institutions. While schools fall into disuse and business streets of small towns deteriorate, churches persist. The documentation of the survival of rural churches and an explanation for it is the goal of our study.

The Study. The data for this study are unique in religious-group literature. They are based on a survey of *all* congregations in 99 rural townships selected randomly statewide.

Missouri is a good location to conduct a study of this kind. The state contains the geographical population center of the U.S., and it reflects a middle position on many national socioeconomic indicators, such as per capita income and level of education. The major metropolitan population centers are at the state's eastern and western edges, in St. Louis and Kansas City. Springfield, the third largest city, is in the southwestern part of the state. This leaves the large middle and southeastern sections without a city as large as 100,000; these areas are comprised of small cities, towns, and families living in the open country.

Geographically and culturally, Missouri is a border state between the North and the South, a bridge between the East and West. It is part of the snowbelt to people living in states to its south, the sunbelt to those to its north. The Ozarks area, in particular, has drawn people from more northern climes as a place for retirement.

Bernard Quinn and associates (1982) have prepared a map color-coded to show the denominations with the largest membership (plurality) for each county in the U.S. Within the borders of Missouri, the solid Baptist majority, found in most of the southeastern and southcentral U.S., shades off. This is not to say

41

that Baptists are not prominent in the state; the map shows them with a plurality in a majority of Missouri counties, but other religious groups are also represented in some counties as plurality denominations. Methodist plurality, which the map shows in a band extending through the center of the U.S. and ending in eastern Colorado, includes counties in northern Missouri. There is a scattering of counties in Missouri in which the plurality is designated as Christian Churches—a combination of the Christian Church (Disciples of Christ), Christian Churches, and Churches of Christ. Roman Catholics are a plurality in a set of contiguous counties extending along the Missouri and Mississippi rivers west and south of St. Louis.

The purpose of placing Missouri in the national religious landscape is to convince ourselves and assure our readers that findings from this research on the rural church have application beyond that state's boundaries.

One more point in our preliminary remarks— we need to clarify what is meant by *rural church*. A church is a local organized religious group that meets for worship on a regular basis; a rural church is one located in a village of less than 2,500 population or in the open country. *Church* and *congregation* are used synonymously in this discussion. The sample for the study consisted of 99 rural townships, with no town as large as 2,500 population within the borders of a township. These were selected randomly and represented about 8 percent of the state's rural townships. Once the 99 townships were selected, all 515 churches within the townships were included in the survey; data were obtained from 492, or 96 percent.

This is the third survey that has used the same sample of townships. The earlier surveys provide a baseline from which to observe change. The interval between the first and last survey was thirty years, with the second survey midway between. Careful attention was given to the wording of questions and categorizations of responses in order to assure comparability among the three surveys. Since the operations of collecting data also bear on comparability, procedures of interviewing and recording data for the three surveys were similar. Personal interviews were conducted with the minister or, if a minister was not available, a church officer.

II

An Overview of Rural Churches

What are rural churches like—not rural Methodist churches, not rural Catholic churches, not rural Assemblies of God—but all the churches in an extensive rural area? Perceptions arise from personal experiences and observations gathered in other ways, but the problem is that we tend to observe only a small corner of a situation. Growing up in a rural community does not guarantee that we have accurate information about rural society or rural churches.

Our earlier windshield survey was an attempt to present a panorama of rural churches; those observations may have been informative, but they were not definitive. Here we provide a detailed map of rural churches in an extensive geographical area—their age, denominational identification, location, size, economic resources, facilities. In addition, selected characteristics of the members are presented.

Age of Churches. Each year some congregations are born, and some die; and some have survived for more than a century. Almost one half (47%) of the existing churches in the survey were founded before 1890; 10 percent, before 1851.

At the end of this chapter, an account is presented of an active congregation established in 1817 (four years before Missouri became a state), reported to be the oldest Disciples of Christ congregation west of the Mississippi River.

Year of Origin of Congregation	Percent of Congregations
Before 1851	10.8
1851 – 1870	11.7
1871 – 1890	24.3
1891 – 1910	13.5
1911 – 1930	9.6
1931 – 1950	13.9
1951 – 1981	16.2

Denominations. The denomination with the largest number of congregations was Southern Baptist, constituting about 24 percent of all congregations about 37 percent of the congregations belonged to the "Baptist family" of churches. The second denomination in number of congregations was Methodist, with 16 percent of the total. Disciples of Christ, Independent Christian Churches, and Churches of Christ each had about 5 percent of the congregations in the rural sample. The above designations accounted for more than two-thirds of all congregations. None of the other denominations had as much as 5 percent of the congregations. The churches in the sample were overwhelmingly Protestant, with only 4 percent Roman Catholic and none Jewish.

Mainline/Nonmainline Churches. Denominations were divided into two broad categories, *mainline* and *nonmainline*. The mainline denominations are more established, and generally participate comfortably in secular society. The denominations designated as mainline were Southern Baptist (there were no American Baptist congregations in the sample), Christian (Disciples of Christ), Episcopal, Federated (and nondenominational) Community Churches, Lutheran, United Methodist, Presbyterian, Roman Catholic, and United Church of Christ. Black Baptist and Methodist churches, although they might have belonged to different national bodies, were classified as mainline congregations. Congregations affiliated with other denominations and independent congregations were classified as nonmainline. Denominations were placed in these categories in the baseline study conducted in 1952, so the same designations were made in the current study in order to make comparisons. Sixty-eight percent of the congregations were affiliated with mainline denominations. These churches were more common in the northern part of the state, where they made up 82 percent of the congregations, compared with 56 percent in the Ozarks and 46 percent in the Bootheel.

The proportion of mainline congregations relative to nonmainline congregations has decreased. In 1952, 74 percent of the congregations were classified as mainline; in 1982, 68 percent.

Location of Congregations. All the churches surveyed were in rural areas (places with population under 2,500). Locations designated as *open country* included places up to 200 population; *small village,* 200–999 population; *large village,* 1,000–2,499. More than half (55%) of the congregations were in open country; 21 percent, in small villages; and 23 percent in large villages.

In the thirty-year period covered by this research, the proportion of churches in open country had declined, with greater concentration of congregations in large villages.

Location	1952	1982
Country	64.2%	54.6%
Small Village	22.5%	21.9%
Large Village	13.3%	23.5%

Congregations in the open country and small villages were more likely to be affiliated with mainline denominations than were congregations in the larger villages. The percentages of mainline congregations were: open country, 70.6 percent; small village, 70.5 percent; large village, 59.1 percent. The larger proportion of mainline churches in open country can be explained historically: Those congregations are likely to be survivors of an earlier rural settlement pattern of open-country neighborhoods, often with a church and/or school. At that time Baptist, Methodist, and Disciples of Christ (which we now classify as mainline) were the most common denominations.

Size of Congregations. Churches in the study were small by almost any standard and were rather evenly distributed among those with roll memberships of under 50, from 50 to 99, and 100 or more. The range of membership was wide, with 3 percent of the congregations reporting 500 or more members, the same percentage that reported fewer than 10 roll members. Membership by size categories had not changed much over the thirty-year period of this study.

Membership	1952	1967	1982
Under 50	32.2%	33.9%	32.4%
50–99	32.4%	29.9%	28.8%
100 or More	35.4%	36.2%	38.9%

Congregations located in large villages tended to have more roll members than those located in the open country and small villages.

Membership	Open Country	Small Village	Large Village
Under 50	38.3%	28.7%	21.6%
50–99	33.0%	23.8%	23.4%
100 or More	28.8%	47.5%	55.0%

Mainline congregations tended to have larger membership than nonmainline congregations. All the Roman Catholic and Missouri Synod Lutheran congregations had more than 100 members, as did a majority of United Church of Christ and Southern Baptist congregations. United Methodist congregations, on the other hand, were almost equally divided among the three size categories. The following tabulation indicates that almost half the mainline congregations had 100 or more members, compared with 20 percent of the nonmainline congregations.

Membership	Mainline	Nonmainline
Under 50	25.4%	47.3%
50–99	27.7%	32.7%
100 or More	47.6%	20.0%

Size as a Resource. Most congregations were entirely self-supporting, without direct financial assistance from their denominations. Per-capita contributions did not vary much by size of membership or by type of church (mainline or nonmainline). Therefore, size of congregation is useful as an index of the resources a congregation has at its disposal. That, of course, is a general rule from which individual churches may depart. Some very small congregations are richly endowed by a single benefactor.

The relationship of resources to the possession of physical facilities of congregations should be fairly direct. Although choices are available about how resources are used, some congregations have so few resources they can barely afford to maintain a simple building and pay modest utility bills. Relationship of resources to programs would appear to be less constraining. Congregations differ in their models of good programs, irrespective of the resources available; however, lack of resources may limit the attainment of desired programs. Thus a congregation might forego benevolences to a children's home in spite of the desire to do so, or it might hold worship services once a month when weekly services would be preferred.

Size is a resource in ways other than providing income. In many congregations, maintenance and upkeep of the church and grounds are carried out by members without compensation, but such work requires a minimum number of able-bodied members. Furthermore, certain programs are not feasible without potential participants. For example, youth groups, young-adult groups, and older-adult groups are not possible without a few people in each of these categories.

Finances. The income of most of the congregations was low: In 1981, almost 80 percent had receipts under $30,000; 43 percent, under $10,000. At the other extreme, about 3 percent had incomes of $100,000 or more for the year.

The largest source of income came from freewill offerings by members of the congregation. One form of freewill offering consisted of taking up a collection at each service to pay the preacher. In most cases, however, giving was more regularized and might include larger periodic (but unpledged) gifts from members.

Annual pledges were a source of income in about 15 percent of the congregations, accounting for most of the income in 7 percent. Other sources of income were bazaars, sales, dinners (14.3% raised money this way), and such special programs as Lord's Acre (2.4% raised money this way).

The largest expenditure of most congregations was for ministers' salaries and other ministerial expenses. Ministers' expenditures, as a part of total expenditures, have been used as an index of appropriate allocations of funds. Lyle Schaller (1982:85) states that some denominational officials see ministers' expenditures of more than 40 percent as a warning signal; and when they exceed 50 percent, it almost always means that other needs are underfinanced. In the rural churches in Missouri, 43 percent exceed the latter criterion.

Ministers' Salaries as a Percent of Total Church Expenditures	Percent of Congregations
Under 10%	9.1%
10–24%	10.0%
25–49%	38.0%
50–74%	34.5%
75% and over	8.4%

Constructing/Maintaining Facilities. The survey question asked whether a church had undergone any renovation (aside from routine maintenance) or new construction in the past 15 years. Sixty-nine percent of the congregations listed such construction:

Type of Renovation	Percent of Congregations
New Church Building	14.7%
Major Addition	12.2%
Separate Structure	4.1%
Major Remodeling	16.1%
Minor Remodeling	6.9%
Special Projects	15.3%
No Renovation/Construction	30.8%

Major remodeling consisted of such things as converting the basement to classrooms and installing restrooms; minor remodeling included such projects as making an outside entrance to the basement or paneling rooms. The most frequent special project was replacing a roof.

The cost of construction and renovation was substantial in many cases. In 8 percent of the congregations that carried out renovations or construction, the cost was $100,000 or more; in 18 percent, $50,000 or more.

Cost of Construction or Renovation	Percent of Congregations Incurring Costs
Under $10,000	45.7%
$10,000–49,000	36.7%
$50,000–99,999	9.4%
$100,000 and over	8.3%

Congregations received little assistance from denominations in covering the costs of construction and renovations—only 11 percent received any assistance, usually in the form of loans. A few received help in planning and fund raising; only seven churches reported building grants from denominations.

Congregations depended on their members for a substantial part of the maintenance, renovation, and repair of facilities. The most commonly hired general maintenance item was mowing of the church grounds, a minor expenditure. Most simple renovations were done by members, while major repairs were more likely to be done by hired workers.

How Would Work Be Done?	General Mainte- nance	Simple Renova- tions	Major Repairs
Volunteer	54.1%	75.6%	34.6%
Hired	40.4%	20.3%	58.6%
Both Hired and Volunteer	5.5%	4.1%	6.8%

Furniture (Material Items and Facilities). With only four exceptions, all the congregations had a church building. Twelve percent of the buildings consisted of a single room, while 16 percent had 11 or more rooms. Material items and facilities varied a great deal. Almost all congregations had a piano, and almost half had an organ. Kitchen and dining facilities were available in about two-thirds. Over one-third provided a parsonage for the minister, about the same percentage that provided a minister's study and had a telephone. Relatively fewer churches had a cemetery adjoining the church (26.5%) or published a newsletter (29.2%).

A case was made earlier for size of congregation as an index of resources. With the exceptions of having a piano and a cemetery adjoining the church, all the facilities are significantly related to size of congregation (Table 2.1). The lack of relationship between size and possession of a piano is explained by the presence of pianos in most congregations; the lack of relationship between size and possession of a cemetery, by the prevalence of cemeteries in open-country churches, which tend to be small.

Overall, nonmainline congregations tended to have fewer facilities than did mainline congregations; however, mainline and nonmainline congregations are not clearly different in this respect when size of congregation is controlled. It follows that resources, as represented by size of congregations, are more important than the type of congregation (mainline or nonmainline) in accounting for the presence or absence of facilities.

We were able to determine changes over the thirty-year period in the presence of selected facilities—kitchen in the church, parsonage, and minister's study in the church. We could do the same for four facilities—piano, organ, dining facilities, and cemetery—over the last fifteen years.

Table 2.1

FACILITIES OF CONGREGATION BY MEMBERSHIP AND TYPE OF CONGREGATION

Roll Membership and Type of Congregation	Percentages of Congregations Having Facilities								
	Telephone	Organ	Piano	Kitchen	Dining Facilities	Cemetery	Study	Parsonage	Newsletter
All Churches	37.3	46.8	90.3	67.8	69.3	26.5	41.8	35.7	29.2
Mainline	38.3	55.1	95.1	74.5	73.6	31.0	42.8	41.1	33.5
Nonmainline	34.9	28.9	79.9	53.0	59.7	16.7	39.5	24.0	19.6
Under 50 Members	13.6	22.7	88.3	46.8	46.1	28.6	22.1	16.9	15.6
Mainline	6.01	22.9	97.6	49.4	48.2	39.8	16.9	10.8	19.3
Nonmainline	22.5	22.5	77.5	43.7	43.7	15.5	28.2	23.9	11.3
50–99 Members	22.1	34.6	91.9	64.0	69.1	25.6	31.7	24.1	17.8
Mainline	13.6	38.6	98.9	67.1	68.2	29.5	26.1	26.1	15.9
Nonmainline	37.5	27.1	79.2	53.3	70.8	18.4	41.7	20.4	21.3
100 Members or More	68.1	76.1	90.8	88.1	88.7	25.4	66.7	60.0	24.9
Mainline	69.7	81.8	91.6	92.3	90.3	27.1	67.1	65.8	51.3
Nonmainline	60.0	46.7	86.7	66.7	80.0	16.7	63.3	30.0	36.7

For facilities observed over the thirty-year period, kitchens and ministers' studies increased quite substantially, while the number of congregations providing a parsonage had not changed much.

Of those facilities for which we had data only for 1967 and 1982, changes had been fairly large for dining facilities and for the possession of an organ; there was little change in possession of a piano or of a cemetery at the site of the church. In the case of a piano, since almost all churches had this instrument in 1967, its presence could hardly increase.

The most general observation is that churches had increased their material possessions and facilities, indicating a rise in the standard of living among congregations. Those facilities that did not increase tended to be explicable in noneconomic terms. Provision of a parsonage for the minister is a traditional practice that is decreasing in popularity. Contemporary practice tends to favor a housing allowance as an alternative to a parsonage. A cemetery on the grounds of the church is also a traditional practice. Church cemeteries are most commonly located at sites of open-country churches, and the number of churches in those locations have tended to decline over the years.

Increases in facilities occurred in each of the size categories of congregations, although larger churches possessed more facilities each time. Thus, small churches as well as large churches were likely to share in the rise in standard of living of congregations.

There were noticeably larger changes for nonmainline than for mainline congregations, especially in regard to those items compared over the thirty-year period (kitchen facilities and ministers' studies). One reason for the high percentage of change for nonmainline groups was their low starting point in 1952. The result is that in facilities, mainline and nonmainline congregations were much more alike in 1982 than they had been thirty years earlier.

Who Are the Members? Most attention in the survey was given to facilities, programs, and organization of rural churches. In addition, however, informants were asked to provide some information about the members.

The vast majority of congregations (91%) had all-white membership; 4 percent had all-black membership; and 5 percent had a mixed black/white membership. In mixed congregations, black members were likely to be in the minority.

Reflecting the demographics of rural Missouri, the typical rural church was weighted with older members and had a majority of female members. In almost one-fifth, half or more of the members were 65 years of age or older; and in three-fifths, 25 percent or more were 65 or older. Women outnumbered men in almost two-thirds of the congregations; men outnumbered women in

3 percent; and the number was about equal in the remainder.

Half or more of the members were retired in almost one-quarter of the congregations. Workers in blue-collar occupations represented a majority of employed members in 38 percent, and farm operators and laborers, in 36 percent. It is of interest that there were no farm-operator members in 22 percent of the congregations. When informants were asked to describe their congregations in terms of members' occupations, 27 percent were described as "farmers' churches," 40 percent as "working persons' churches," 2 percent as "professional persons' churches," 11 percent as "retired persons' churches," and 20 percent as "other types." The "other types" category was usually a combination of the above descriptions.

There are certain differences in characteristics of members of mainline and nonmainline congregations. Mainline congregations tended to have an older membership: 67 percent of mainline congregations, compared with 47 percent of nonmainline congregations, reported that 25 percent or more of their members were 65 or older.

The principal difference between mainline and nonmainline congregations commented on in the literature is socioeconomic status. In rural Missouri, members of mainline congregations tended to have higher status, as measured by occupation. Some members of 58 percent of mainline congregations, compared with 48 percent of nonmainline, fell into the U.S. census' highest socioeconomic-status category (professionals, owners and managers of large businesses, government officials). The greater occupational difference, however, was between blue-collar workers and farm operators. Mainline congregations were twice as likely as nonmainline congregations to have a majority of employed members as farm operators—42 percent and 22 percent respectively. Nonmainline congregations were twice as likely to have a majority of blue-collar workers—57 percent and 29 percent respectively.

We can account, in part, for these occupational differences by considering the time and circumstances of the establishment of the churches. Mainline congregations were much more likely than nonmainline congregations to have been started before the turn of the century; 61 percent of mainline congregations, compared with 18 percent of the nonmainline, were founded by 1890. Their founding coincided with the domination of agriculture in rural Missouri; and tradition, associated with stable families in neighborhoods, has helped them survive. At the same time, although the number of farms has decreased and the number employed in agriculture has declined, stable families and elite members of the community are often farm families.

In contrast, 59 percent of the nonmainline congregations, compared with 16 percent of the mainline, were founded after 1930. Occupations of the rural population have become more diverse, and rural areas have seen a certain amount of immigration of persons with different socioeconomic backgrounds. Nonmainline congregations did not have much claim on farm families who tended to have deep roots in the community (including religious affiliation), but they did have a chance to attract unattached newcomers, at least some of whom had previous experience with that particular denomination or a similar one.

On a broader basis, socioeconomic differences of members in mainline and nonmainline congregations may not be as great in rural communities as in urban communities. Hart Nelsen and Raymond Potvin (1977:110), for example, comment that rural Protestant churches are more class-inclusive than their counterparts in urban areas. Most rural communities do not have a large enough pool of professionals and upper white-collar workers to form elite-membership congregations. On the other hand, churches in urban areas can do exactly that, and can appeal to more finely drawn groups over the entire socioeconomic range. The attenuation of differences between mainline and nonmainline congregations can also be accounted for in part by the denominational mix in each of the categories. Both the mainline and nonmainline denominations with the largest number of congregations were located toward the center of the mainline-nonmainline continuum. For mainline denominations, these were Southern Baptist and Disciples of Christ; for nonmainline denominations, "other" Baptist, independent Christian Churches, Churches of Christ, and Assemblies of God.

The Ashland Neighborhood Christian Church

One of the congregations in our study is reported to be the oldest Christian Church (Disciples of Christ) congregation west of the Mississippi River. It dates from 1817; the present building was constructed in 1914. The church is located in the open country of Howard County. Rural sociologist Edmund de S. Brunner (1917) gives the following account of the early congregation:

Everyone of its few members came to the services on horseback, the men in blue jeans and the women in calico or linsey and sunbonnets. It was the community's one meeting-place—a primitive social center— and the people came from miles around to listen to sermons two hours long and to enjoy a chat with the neighbors. It was rough structure of unhewn logs, chinked and daubed with mud. For fifty years this building stood and served the community. Within its walls rang the rude but powerful eloquence of the circuit-rider. The yellow records tell of the ban on the "gay fantastic" and of the prohibition of violin music as "kharnal." The next church was a roomy building of the household farmers' type, which burned down in 1913.

Brunner was not the only sociologist to comment on the Ashland neighborhood and its church. Carl C. Taylor and E. W. Lehmann (1920) did a study of the Ashland neighborhood in which the church figured prominently. They reported:

The present church edifice is a beautiful brick structure which with its total equipment cost $14,500 [in 1914]. It is recognized as a "community building." A four-year subscription high school is housed in its basement. It was being used as a Red Cross work room at the time of the survey. All agricultural club meetings, road meetings, literary meetings or other community enterprises center in this building.

The church is about equidistant from the three chief trading centers, being eight miles from Rocheport, eight miles from New Franklin and seven and a half miles from Fayette. . . . There are no hard-surface roads in the community, though the roads are almost universally well dragged. Only one farmer asserted that his road to market was really "bad." Six more of them had some portion of the road which was only "fair." All others designated their roads to market as "good." It should be noted, however, that it is of little use to attempt to hold a community meeting of any type at certain seasons of the year or immediately after a rain storm, for practically all these people travel in automobiles and can not come over the dirt roads at such times. Hard-surfaced roads would do much to improve the life and conditions of the community.

Membership figures were not given in that early survey, but the 1982 survey shows that the membership on the roll numbers 38, about half of whom are 65 years of age or over. The congregation has worship services two Sundays a month, conducted by a minister who serves two other congregations, both of which are larger. Problems of the congregation do not appear to be financial, because support is reported to be good; the problems involve attracting new members from among an aging local population.

Summary

Nestled in the neighborhoods and communities, many rural churches have a long history, some even preceding the organization of the state. Denominations of the frontier—Baptist, Methodist, and Christian—predominate. Churches categorized as mainline are more numerous than nonmainline churches, and they tend to be larger. However, nonmainline churches are growing in number, while there are losses in mainline churches. This trend is not unique to rural Missouri churches, but is occurring throughout the U.S.

Rural Missouri churches have not abandoned the open country; it was the location of more than half of them in 1982. Congregations so located were smaller than those in the villages; they were also over-represented by mainline denominations. From the perspective of the thirty years covered in this research, some movement of congregations from open country to larger villages was observed. Do not expect to find losses of congregations in the larger villages; there both mainline and nonmainline congregations had increased in number over the period covered by this study.

Congregations ranged widely in size from 10 members or fewer to 500 members or more, but most were small. Size is an important consideration, because congregations depended almost entirely on their members for economic support and to carry on their programs. The small size of congregations is reflected in their low financial capability and, in turn, their modest facilities. It was noted, however, that over the thirty years of observation, facilities of congregations had increased. The increase was most noteworthy in nonmainline congregations. Starting in 1952 at a decided disadvantage, by 1982 nonmainline congregations were about equal, in facilities and material items, to mainline congregations of the same size.

Few black or racially mixed congregations were found among the churches studied. In most congregations, women outnumbered men, and the membership was weighted toward older persons. Many of the members were retired; of those employed, farmers and blue-collar workers were most numerous. Mainline congregations were more likely to have farmers as a majority of their employed members, while in nonmainline congregations, it was likely to be blue-collar workers. The explanation for this difference is strongly related to the time and circumstances of the establishment of each congregation.

III

Changes in the Number of Congregations

Among the questions that come to mind when we think seriously about rural churches is this: Can they survive? The fear that many may not seems reasonable when we consider the institutional and ecological changes taking place—the urbanization of rural society. If the past portends the future, however, we can be fairly certain that aggregate survival is not in doubt. We have monitored the births and deaths of congregations in the same area sample of rural Missouri for a period of thirty years, and over that time, the net loss of congregations has been small. This suggests that the rural church as an institution is not in jeopardy.

Aggregate survival experience, however, is not the same for all categories of churches. As we show in this chapter, the size of the congregation, the location of the congregation (with respect to size of place, area of the state, and population change of the township), and the type of congregation (mainline/nonmainline) make a difference in survival. Aggregate survival of churches is better among large than small congregations, in large villages than open country, in the Ozarks than the Commercial Agricultural Area or the Bootheel, in townships with population increases than in townships with population decreases, and in nonmainline than mainline congregations.

Optimism is expressed by rural ministers and church leaders about the future of their churches. Informants representing 62 percent of the congregations in the sample thought their churches would grow in the next ten years, and an additional 22 percent thought membership would not change appreciably. Eleven percent expected a loss of membership; an additional 5 percent expected their churches to close. By a margin of 78 to 55 percent, informants for nonmainline churches were more optimistic about growth than were their mainline counterparts. Size of congregation was much more a factor in positive assessment of the future for mainline congregations than it was for nonmainline congregations. Thirty-eight percent of the informants for small mainline congregations thought they would grow, compared with 70 percent for large mainline congregations. In contrast, a large majority of informants (70% or more) for each size category of nonmainline congregations expected growth.

Losses and Gains of Congregations. Details of losses and gains in number of congregations are shown in Table 3.1. The first panel in the table shows changes in the fifteen-year period 1952–1967; the second panel, in the fifteen-year period

Table 3.1

GAINS AND LOSSES OF RELIGIOUS CONGREGATIONS DURING A THIRTY-YEAR PERIOD BY TYPE OF CONGREGATION

Congregations	All	Mainline	Non-mainline
Number in 1952	547	400	147
Losses 1952 to 1967	69	47	22
Gains 1952 to 1967	50	19	31
Net Change 1952 to 1967	-19	-28	+9
% Net Change 1952 to 1967	-3.6	-7.0	+6.1
Number in 1967	528	372	156
Losses 1967 to 1982	61	36	25
Gains 1967 to 1982	48	9	39
Net Change 1967 to 1982	-13	-27	+14
% Net Change 1967 to 1982	-2.5	-7.3	+9.0
Number in 1982	515	345	170
Losses 1952 to 1982	130	83	47
Gains 1952 to 1982	98	28	70
Net Change 1952 to 1982	-32	-55	+23
% Net Change 1952 to 1982	-5.9	-13.8	+15.6

1967–1982. The third panel shows changes for the entire thirty-year period, 1952–1982. In looking at the two fifteen-year periods, we can observe whether rates and directions of changes were the same or different for the two periods. After determining the general trends, we will relate changes in congregations to size of congregations, type of congregations (mainline or nonmainline), area of the state, size of places in which the church is located, and change in township population.

The loss in number of congregations was about 6 percent for the thirty-year period. Losses of congregations were at a somewhat higher rate for the first than for the second fifteen-year period. These figures, which indicate only small changes, mask the dynamics of religious groups in the study area. During the thirty years, 130 congregations ceased to exist, and 98 new congregations were formed. In fact, there must have been more change than that; congregations undoubtedly were started and lost within the two fifteen-year periods, and therefore were undetected in the surveys.

Data available for the period 1967 to 1982 (the same data were not available for the period 1952 to 1967) provide more details about the nature of losses. Sixty-one congregations present in 1967 were not in the sample area in 1982. Of those, 29 (47.5%) had disbanded; 19 (31.1%) had merged with another congregation; 6 (9.8%) had relocated outside the sample area; and definite information was unavailable for 7 (11.5%), although they probably had disbanded, rather than merged or relocated. Mainline congregations, accounting for 14 of the 19 mergers, were more likely than nonmainline congregations to follow the merger route. Seven of the fourteen mainline mergers were Methodist congregations; three were Presbyterian; three were Disciples of Christ; and one was a Community Church. Most mergers seemed to be a means of closing very small churches; only two of the nineteen merged churches were reported to have a membership of thirty or more. In general, most congregations were very small at the time of loss to the area: 81 percent had fewer than thirty members; 60 percent, fewer than twenty.

Changes by Size of Congregation. Size of congregation was an important variable in the survival of congregations from 1952 to 1982. Small size in 1952, however, did not necessarily doom a congregation. Of the 162 congregations with under fifty members in 1952, 77, or 48 percent, were still active in 1982. The majority of the small-category survivors remained at less than fifty members (60%), while 31 percent had advanced to the next size category of 50–99 members, and 9 percent had 100 or more members. However, chances for survival for the thirty-year period were much better for congregations with 50–99 members, and even better for those with 100 or more—the percentages were 76 and 90 percent respectively. Among the 1952 middle-size congregations (50–99 members) that were still active thirty years later, 36 percent remained in the same size category, 34 percent declined to fewer than 50 members, and 30 percent increased to 100 or more. Of the congregations in the largest size category surviving until 1982, 71 percent still had more than 100 members, with 19 percent and 10 percent, respectively, falling to the two lower size categories.

Changes by Type of Congregation. Considerable differences in the patterns of change for mainline and nonmainline congregations are shown in Table 3.1. Mainline congregations, more numerous than nonmainline congregations, have shown a net loss of 14 percent over the thirty-year period, while nonmainline congregations have shown a net gain of 16 percent, and this general pattern persists for each of the two fifteen-year periods. The rate of loss for mainline congregations was almost identical for each of the periods, while the rate of increase of nonmainline congregations was somewhat greater in the second period.

If we look more closely at the actual openings and closings of congregations, we see that nonmainline congregations are more volatile than mainline congregations—that is, they not only gained more congregations, they also lost more congregations, relative to their base number. This was true for both fifteen-year periods; in the second period (1967 to 1982), compared with the first period (1952 to 1967), both losses and gains were reduced for mainline congregations, while both losses and gains increased for nonmainline congregations. Thus a specific mainline congregation in 1952 was less at risk of closing during the next thirty years than was a specific nonmainline congregation.

Changes by Rural Social Areas. As described earlier, the three rural social areas (RSAs) of Missouri are the Commercial Agricultural Area of northern and western Missouri, the Ozarks area, and the southeastern Mississippi Delta area known as the Bootheel. The Commercial Agricultural Area had the largest percentage of mainline congregations; the Bootheel, the smallest. In 1952, the percentages of mainline congregations in the three RSAs were: Commercial Agricultural Area, 84 percent; Ozarks, 63 percent; and the Bootheel, 49 percent. In 1982 the percentages were: Commercial Agricultural Area, 82 percent; Ozarks, 56 percent; and the Bootheel, 46 percent.

During the thirty-year period (1952 to 1982), only the Ozarks area had an overall net gain in congregations. There was a net loss among mainline congregations in each of the rural social areas: Commercial Agricultural Area, −16 percent; Ozarks, −9 percent; the Bootheel, −18 percent. Only the Bootheel showed a net loss of nonmainline congregations for the same period; the figures for changes among nonmainline congregations were: Commercial Agricultural Area, +9 percent; Ozarks, +29 percent; and Bootheel, −7 percent.

Although the Commercial Agricultural Area had relatively few nonmainline congregations in 1952, nonmainline congregations increased in that area about 9 percent between 1952 and 1982. Furthermore, this increase is accounted for by the 14 percent increase in the most recent fifteen-year period (1967 to 1982), which countered a 4 percent net loss in the earlier fifteen-year period (1952 to 1967). The figures suggest an invasion (in the ecological sense) of the Commercial Agricultural Area by nonmainline congregations.

In the Ozarks, by contrast, while there has been a substantial increase in nonmainline congregations, the greater increase came in the first fifteen-year period; there was an 18 percent increase from 1952 to 1967, compared with a 9 percent increase in 1967 to 1982. In the last fifteen-year period, the increase in number of nonmainline congregations was relatively greater in the Commercial Agricultural Area than in the Ozarks—14 percent and 9 percent respectively.

Changes by Size of Location. The 1952 study placed religious groups in three categories, according to size of the place they were located: (1) open country (under 200 population); (2) small village (200–999); and (3) large village (1,000–2,499). Of the total number of churches in 1952, 64 percent were in the open country, 22 percent in small villages, and 13 percent in large villages. In 1982, 55 percent were in the open country, 22 percent in small villages, and 24 percent in large villages. During the thirty-year period, 80 percent of the closures, contrasted with 53 percent of the new churches, took place in the open country; thus a wide gap occurred between openings and closings of churches in the open country. In contrast, large villages were the sites of only 7 percent of the closures, compared with 28 percent of new churches. Over the three decades, there were more new religious congregations established in the small and large villages than there were closures. Thus in net terms, all the losses of congregations occurred in the open country.

Mainline and nonmainline open-country congregations showed losses between 1952 and 1967, as well as between 1967 and 1982. A net loss of mainline groups and a net gain of nonmainline groups in the small villages occurred during both time periods. In the large villages, there was a net gain of both mainline and nonmainline congregations in both time periods.

In comparing the changes in church locations during the two time periods, it is evident that the pattern of change observed between 1952 and 1967 continued at a faster pace between 1967 and 1982. As a result, the small and large villages were experiencing a net gain in churches, while the open country was experiencing a net loss.

Changes in Number of Congregations, Related to Population Changes in Townships. We recorded the population changes of the 99 surveyed townships from 1950 to 1970 and from 1970 to 1980. The division was made at that point, because it was the U.S. census date closest to the dates of the surveys—1952, 1967, and 1982. This division point is particularly useful, because at about 1970, a trend occurred that saw population increases in many rural areas of the nation, a trend evident to some degree in the rural population of Missouri. However, not all rural areas of the state shared in the increases. Some (15) of the sample townships showed a population increase for both periods, 1950 to 1970 and 1970 to 1980; others (37) had a population decrease for both periods, a few (3) grew during the first period and lost during the second; and a substantial number of townships (44) lost population between 1950 and 1970, but gained between 1970 and 1980. In townships with population increases that extended over both periods, new congregations (29) exceeded losses of congregations (15) by about two to one; the opposite was true in townships that had lost population during both periods, where losses of congregations (51) exceeded new congregations (12) by about four to one. For the townships that had lost population between 1950 and 1970 but gained population between 1970 and 1980, the losses (61) and additions (54) more nearly balanced each other. The townships that had grown in the first period and lost in the second also showed a balance of additions (3) and losses (3) of congregations, but the number of townships and congregations was too small to calculate reliable results. Overall, a rather substantial relationship existed between population change in townships and gains or losses of congregations.

Summary

The first and perhaps the central conclusion to be drawn from observations over a period of three decades is that the rural church in aggregate is not in jeopardy of demise. Beyond that, in a general way, losses and gains of congregations make sense when placed in the context of changes in the ecology and population of an urbanizing rural society. These losses and gains were in the same direction as changes in other institutional organizations and in the expected direction with regard to population changes. This is exemplified by comparing rural schools and rural churches. The direction is the same, but differences in the rates of change are large. The number of congregations has declined, but the decline has been modest compared to rural schools. Churches have a reduced, but still substantial, presence in the open country, which schools have almost completely abandoned. Mainline congregations were more likely than nonmainline congregations to show losses. For mainline, increases occurred only in the large villages; for nonmainline congregations, increases occurred in both small and large villages. This suggests, at least, that mainline congregations parallel changes in other institutional organizations in rural society more closely than do nonmainline congregations. This is in agreement with the idea that mainline congregations are more in the mainstream of secular society and therefore more sensitive to societal changes.

More complicated and not as easily documented are the effects of changes in the labor force and the effects of new entrants to rural

75

areas on rural churches. These changes result in a more socioeconomically diverse population, one less dependent on agricultural employment. The urbanization of rural society as indexed by greater occupational diversity suggests finer divisions among religious groups that appeal to particular socioeconomic sectors of the community. Increases in nonmainline congregations may reflect the religious preferences of a more diverse rural population.

Finally, the expected relationship at the township level exists between population change, and gains and losses of congregations. Those townships that gained population over the entire period were more likely to have a net gain of congregations; the opposite was true in townships that showed population loss over the entire period.

Overall, we found that changes in the number of rural congregations and the distribution of gains and losses between mainline and nonmainline congregations were compatible with ecological and population changes in rural Missouri, but not highly sensitive to them. In order to understand the attenuation of responsiveness of congregations to obvious ecological and population factors, we need to give attention to the organizational characteristics of rural churches, and to the relationships of rural congregations to their communities and the social structures of the larger society. These topics are considered in the following chapters.

IV

Programs and Organizations

Programs and the ways they are structured are the organizational heart of a congregation. Even from casual observation, we know that there are substantial differences among congregations. Stemming from denominational affiliations, congregations vary in their preferred models of services, programs, and internal organizations. The division between mainline and nonmainline churches captures some of these differences. Congregations also differ on the basis of available resources—both human and financial—and size captures some of these differences. In addition to differences among congregations, we will consider *changes* in program and organization that have occurred over the three decades of this study. Has the urbanization of rural society brought major changes to this aspect of congregational life? Based on this continuing urbanization, we might expect that congregations would take on a more bureaucratic form that would include greater internal complexity and formalization of activities.

Observation of the effects of denominational differences (as indicated by mainline/nonmainline), resources (as indicated by size), and urbanization (as indicated by changes in complexity and formalization) is like watching a juggler keep three balls in the air; we can observe the whole pattern of the performance, but it is difficult to follow the paths of the individual balls. We have cross-tabulated size and type (mainline/nonmainline) of congregations and, where possible, made comparisons for 1952, 1967, and 1982. In reporting the results, we emphasize patterns rather than the twists and turns of the data. For example, where the effects of size on programs and organization are stated, they are based on a tabulation of this variable, though the details of the table are not shown.

Religious Services. Churches in rural Missouri emphasized the worship service. Most congregations held weekly Sunday morning worship services, and almost all had Sunday school programs. Additional congregation-wide services were conducted; Sunday evening and midweek services, and annual revivals were quite common.

The Sunday morning worship service is the centerpiece of local churches' programs. To the common query, "When do you have church?" the answer given is the time of the worship service (e.g., every Sunday at 11:00 A.M.). In many congregations, the *form* of the service is repeated from week to week, with only slight variations. The pattern is likely to include corporate prayer, hymns by the congregation and music by a choir, Scripture reading, and, as the focus of the service, the minister's sermon, closely tied to the service's framework.

The services of some congregations, on the other hand, are quite unstructured in form and are open-ended. One minister said a service might last as long as four hours, although most are shorter. His comment was, "When people get to shoutin' for the Lord, you don't want to turn them off." John Earle and his associates point out that the services of many sectarian congregations "appear faintly contrived, a form of 'patterned spontaneity,' in which people respond to cues and appeals in a consistent way" (Earle et al.: 1976).

In rural Missouri, 86 percent of the congregations held worship services at least once a week; the most common alternative pattern was every other week, or the second and fourth Sunday, with 10 percent following this pattern.

Many rural congregations continue to have congregation-wide services in addition to the regular Sunday morning service. Over half the congregations (56%) had Sunday evening services. Midweek services were also quite common, with Wednesday evening being the most popular time; more than half the congregations (51%) held such services. Revivals were a regular—usually an annual—activity in many congregations. Revivals seek to renew commitments of members, bring people back to the church, and gain new members. Today's revivals, however, are usually pale imitations of the "old time" revivals and camp meetings characteristic of frontier religion. They usually consist of evening services, often led by visiting evangelists, and emphasize singing and exhortative preaching. Sixty percent of the congregations reported a revival program during the past year. The most common length of a revival was seven days, followed by six days.

A tabulation of religious services by size and type of congregation indicates a modest rise in weekly Sunday morning worship services as size of church increased; 98 percent of large congregations, compared with 83 percent of middle-sized and 74 percent of small congregations, had services at least once a week. But the patterns for mainline and nonmainline congregations were quite different. Size made little difference for nonmainline congregations; almost all, large and small, held weekly Sunday morning worship services. Size, however, made a substantial difference for mainline congregations; 54 percent of the smallest congregations, compared with 76 percent of the medium-sized and 97 percent of the largest congregations, had weekly worship services. If size is regarded as a resource, the interpretation of these different patterns is that programs of mainline congregations are more sensitive to differences in resources than are programs of nonmainline congregations. For example, nonmainline congregations may be less dependent on professionally trained clergy and therefore are not so constrained by their inability to engage a full-time minister.

The relationship of size and type of congregation to Sunday evening services, midweek services, and revivals is similar to that for Sunday morning worship services. Nonmainline congregations are much more likely to hold these services, and size does not make much difference. Among mainline congregations, size does influence whether or not these services are held.

Changes in congregation-wide services were observed by considering their presence at three points over a thirty-year period—1952, 1967, 1982. The most impressive change was the proportion of congregations having worship services every week, which increased from 45 percent in 1952 to 86 percent in 1982. At all three points of time, nonmainline congregations were more likely than mainline congregations to have weekly worship services. Since nonmainline congregations were likely to have weekly services whether they were small or large, the increases were most pronounced in the small- and middle-sized mainline congregations.

Frequency of congregations holding midweek services had not changed much over the years of observation. Comparing data for 1952 and 1967, it appeared that this type of service was on the decline, especially for nonmainline groups. That trend, however, did not continue between 1967 and 1982, and losses in the first period were made up in the second, for most categories of mainline/nonmainline type and size. A gradual reduction took place in the proportion of congregations having revivals. This reduction was very uniform, in that the decline from 1952 to 1967 continued from 1967 to 1982, for almost all mainline/nonmainline size categories. We did not have 1952 data for Sunday evening services, but between 1967 and 1982, the percentage of congregations conducting these services was almost unchanged. There were no notable changes for any of the mainline/nonmainline size categories.

Overall, the greatest change in religious services was the substantial increase in congregations that held weekly Sunday morning worship services. Because the change had been much more in mainline than nonmainline congregations, these two types of congregations were more alike in this characteristic in 1982 than in 1952. Other types of religious services did not match the increase of congregations holding weekly religious services; there was little change in the percentages having midweek services, revivals, and Sunday evening services.

Suborganizations in Congregations. Its number of suborganizations is an indication of a congregation's organizational complexity. More complex organizations tend to require greater formalization in management and attention to administration. Congregations' organizational patterns differ in model and in reality, depending on denominational standards and membership resources. For example, a congregation of a structured denomination such as The United Methodist Church would be expected to have an internal organization that conforms to denominational prescription; however, membership size may alter the forms of internal organization, such as the number of committees or kinds of groups. If there are few or no young people in the congregation, it is not feasible to have a youth organization. Some types of suborganizations such as Sunday school, women's organizations, youth organizations, and choirs are common; others, such as young-adults' and older-adults' organizations, are relatively rare. Suborganizations, by type of congregation for 1952, 1967, and 1982, are shown in Table 4.1.

Sunday Schools. Sunday schools traditionally have been a central part of rural church programs and, except for worship services, are the most common activity of the congregation. Some denominations call the common Sunday school hour Church school or Bible study, among other names. If worship services are not conducted weekly, the Sunday school often substitutes as a Sunday gathering and service. The Sunday school director is often a key person in the congregation and may hold long tenure. Most absences of Sunday schools among congregations in the study can be accounted for by Catholic and Primitive Baptist churches, which do not include such an organization in their models.

Table 4.1

SPECIFIC SUBORGANIZATIONS BY TYPE OF
CONGREGATION, 1952, 1967, 1982

| Type of Suborganization | Percentage of Congregations with Suborganizations | | |
	1952	1967	1982
Sunday School			
Total	88.8	91.5	93.3
Mainline	87.9	92.2	94.3
Nonmainline	90.8	89.7	91.1
Women's Organization			
Total	56.5	56.2	52.3
Mainline	72.0	66.6	62.3
Nonmainline	20.5	30.8	31.2
Youth Organization			
Total	37.6	39.4	38.3
Mainline	44.2	43.2	39.2
Nonmainline	18.9	30.1	36.3
*Study Group**			
Total	——	——	42.3
Mainline	——	——	45.2
Nonmainline	——	——	35.8
Choir			
Total	35.6	40.7	43.6
Mainline	42.9	33.7	50.6
Nonmainline	15.2	16.4	28.7
Men's Organization			
Total	12.9	15.8	17.5
Mainline	17.0	21.2	21.9
Nonmainline	1.5	2.7	8.3
Young-Adults' Organization			
Total	8.0	7.0	9.2
Mainline	10.0	8.6	10.5
Nonmainline	2.3	4.1	6.4
Older-Adults' Organization			
Total	2.6	5.0	4.7
Mainline	3.5	2.9	5.4
Nonmainline	0.0	2.7	3.2

*Data for study group not available for 1952 and 1967.

Sunday school programs were present in 93 percent of the congregations. The range was narrow, from 86 percent for small mainline congregations to 97 percent for large congregations. Large mainline and nonmainline congregations had identical percentages.

Women's Organization. Women's organizations are the most common suborganization, with the exception of Sunday school. Traditionally, women's groups have engaged in money-making activities such as bazaars and dinners. The presence of women's organizations is related to size of the congregation, and they are significantly more common in mainline than nonmainline congregations, in all but the smallest size category.

Choir. Choirs were the third most common suborganization and were quite closely related to size of congregation, present in 20 percent, 34 percent, and 73 percent of the small, medium, and large congregations, respectively. The differences between mainline and nonmainline congregations within size categories were relatively small. The presence of a choir, then, appears to be more sensitive to size than to type. A problem for small congregations in maintaining a choir, as with other suborganizations, is simply having a sufficient number of people to participate.

Study Group. Study groups are variable from congregation to congregation. They commonly are devoted to Bible study but may consider other topics, such as social issues. There appears to be some overlap between study groups and adult Sunday school classes. The presence of study groups was related to size of congregation but not to the mainline/nonmainline division.

Youth Organization. The presence of a youth organization is related to size of congregation, ranging from 20 percent of the small congregations to 65 percent of the large congregations. Reversing the pattern between mainline and nonmainline in previous suborganizations, more nonmainline small and medium-sized congregations had youth organizations than did their mainline counterparts. For the larger congregations, the proportions of mainline and nonmainline congregations with youth organizations were almost identical.

Men's Organization. A few small or medium-sized congregations and about one-third of the large congregations had a men's organization. Among the larger congregations, men's organizations were more common among mainline than among nonmainline congregations.

Young-adults' and Older-adults' Organizations. Few congregations had young-adults' or older-adults' organizations—10 percent and 5 percent respectively. They tended to be found in larger congregations when they did occur, and there were no significant differences between mainline and nonmainline congregations, either as a whole or within size categories.

Total Number of Suborganizations. The number of suborganizations in each congregation was counted. The total number, as was true of the individual suborganizations, was related to size of congregation. Among smaller and medium-sized congregations, there were no substantial differences between mainline and nonmainline congregations in number of suborganizations; in larger congregations, mainline congregations were likely to have more suborganizations.

Total Divisions of Suborganizations. Complexity of suborganizations was examined further by accounting for the number of divisions within suborganizations. For example, Sunday schools characteristically had several classes, women's organizations were sometimes divided into "circles," and there might be more than one choir. Any suborganization could have more than one division. Size of congregation was an important factor in accounting for the number of divisions of suborganizations, but type of congregations was not. When size was controlled, the number of divisions was similar for mainline and nonmainline congregations.

Our overall conclusion from an examination of suborganizations is that size is a good predictor of organizational complexity, but type of congregation as indicated by the mainline/nonmainline division is not.

Changes in Suborganization. With the exception of "study groups," we can determine the changes in percentages of congregations that reported specific suborganizations from 1952 to 1967 and from 1967 to 1982. A general observation is that the percentages of congregations having each of the suborganizations was very similar for each of the three points of time. A change that appears to be significant is that for most suborganizations, differences between mainline and nonmainline congregations were less in 1982 than in 1952. For women's organizations and youth organizations, this shift resulted from a smaller percentage of mainline congregations and a larger percentage of nonmainline congregations reporting those suborganizations in 1982. Youth organizations clearly illustrate this tendency. In 1952, mainline congregations were more than twice as likely as nonmainline to have a youth organization—44 percent and 19 percent respectively; between 1952 and 1982, the percentage of mainline congregations reporting a youth organization declined modestly, from 44 percent to 39 percent. The gain among nonmainline congregations was much greater—from 19 percent to 36 percent. By 1982, the percentages were about the same.

For choirs, men's organizations, young-adults' organizations, and older-adults' organizations, the percentages rose from 1952 to 1982 for both mainline and nonmainline congregations. However, the rise was greater for nonmainline congregations, resulting in greater similarity between the two types in 1982 than in 1952.

Formalization. Together with organizational complexity, formalization of certain practices reveals the characteristics of a congregation's internal organization. As indexes of the formalization of practices, inquiry was made as to whether congregations raised money by annual pledges, and had a written agreement with their ministers. Only 15 percent of the congregations raised a part of their budgets through pledges, and about one-third had a formal contract or agreement with their minister. Size of congregation was not statistically related to whether either of these practices was followed. Type of congregation was related only to the greater likelihood that ministers of mainline congregations would have a written contract in small- and medium-sized churches, but not in large congregations.

The indexes are available only for 1967 and 1982. At both times, the proportions of congregations using pledges to raise money were low, and when all congregations were considered, they were identical. During the fifteen-year period, somewhat fewer mainline congregations and somewhat more nonmainline congregations usd pledges. By the end of the period, the proportion of mainline and nonmainline congregations using this method of fund raising was almost the same. As was the case with pledges, identical percentages of congregations had formal contracts with ministers in 1967 and 1982. Size was not much of a factor at either time. The practice, though, was much more common among mainline than among nonmainline congregations; that gap was not effectively lessened over time, except in congregations in the largest size category.

On the basis of these indexes, there is little evidence that congregations are becoming more formal in relationship with their ministers or in funding. The only qualification is that there may be a slight movement toward greater formalization among larger nonmainline congregations.

Summary

Rural congregations emphasize worship services; they tend to be simply organized, as indicated by relatively few suborganizations. There was little evidence of formalization of activities as indexed by pledges for fund raising or by formal contracts for ministers.

Programs and elements of internal organization were, with few exceptions, related to size of congregations. Partial exceptions to this rule were found among nonmainline congregations, where there is not much relation between size and frequency of congregation-wide services (Sunday morning worship services, Sunday evening and midweek services, and revivals). In mainline congregations, size did not appear to be a factor in whether or not a formal contract was extended to the minister, while it was a factor in nonmainline congregations.

Substantial differences occurred between mainline and nonmainline congregations in the area of congregation-wide services, with such services more frequent for nonmainline congregations, and in the area of a minister having a contract, with this practice more common in mainline congregations. There was little or no difference between the two types of congregations in complexity of internal organization as indexed by suborganizations, when size of congregation was controlled.

Several generalizations can be made about *changes* in programs and internal organization of rural congregations over the past thirty (sometimes fifteen) years. First, and it cannot be overemphasized, changes in these organizational areas have been modest. Programs and internal organization of churches in rural Missouri in 1982 were much like they had been in 1967 and in 1952. No revolution occurred in the organization of this social institution.

In what can probably be described as a "rise in the level of living" of congregations, a substantially larger proportion of congregations in 1982 than in 1952 was able to provide themselves with a program of weekly Sunday morning worship services. On the other hand, there was little evidence that congregations are becoming more (or less) complex and bureaucratic in their internal structures. Considering all congregations, the frequency of suborganizations was similar at each of the three survey times. Furthermore, there seemed to be no greater formalization of activities as indicated by use of pledges to raise money or by having formal contracts with ministers. The effects of urbanization, suggested at the beginning of this discussion of programs and internal organization, do not seem to have occurred.

Observations of relatively small changes in the complexity of programs and internal organization of congregations mask, to some extent, the variable changes in mainline and nonmainline churches. On some items of program and internal organization, both types changed in the same direction, with nonmainline congregations moving more than mainline congregations. On other items, mainline and nonmainline congregations moved in opposite directions toward each other—typically a decrease among mainline congregations and an increase among nonmainline. The effect of both of these kinds of movement has been to substantially reduce differences in organizational complexity between mainline and nonmainline congregations.

V

External Relationships

Communities are composed of individuals and organizations which interact with one another in carrying out everyday activities. They are the sociocultural environments of churches, and churches are actors in communities. Religious groups relate to their particular communities in culturally defined ways. They are expected to declare positions of right and wrong behavior on the basis of a system of beliefs. In a very real sense, congregations depend upon their communities for support: A congregation draws members from a limited geographical area and depends almost entirely upon that membership for its financial support and program participants.

On the cultural level, churches are enmeshed in the values and behavior norms of their communities. Applicable to Missouri churches are Samuel Hill's comments on the southern church, which he describes as "comfortable in its homeland, and the culture fits comfortably with the church." Hill attributes this to the "subjective orientation and democratic polity" of the churches and notes that both church and culture have a rural value-tone and practice a "folksy" fellowship (Hill 1966:30). Social and cultural distance between clergy and church members of Missouri rural churches tends to be small.

Ministers' common responses to the question, "What are the main satisfactions of a rural ministry?" were variations of the response of a United Methodist minister: "Working closely with people on a personal basis—they respond more than a sophisticated congregation." In the same community, a minister of a Christian (Disciples of Christ) congregation responded: "The honesty of the people in everything—old-fashioned ethics. What affects the community affects the church and vice versa." Embedded in the values of the local community, congregations may reject or alter positions of the denominations on moral and social issues; examples are found in such areas as foreign aid, racial integration, and gender equality.

Tradition and collective memory are important elements in many congregations; it would be difficult to understand the survival of some small congregations without resorting to these factors. St. Joseph parish near Mendon is a mission of St. Bonaventure parish in Marceline, Missouri. A story in *The Catholic Missourian* (Yates: 1987) reports that "with no resident priest, the parishioners tend to take responsibility for and care of their people and church." The church is a white wooden structure in the open country. "Forty families make up the St. Joseph parish family, many of them named Gladback, descendants of Henrick Gladback who came from Grofen on the Rhine in Germany in 1856. Large families, many of whom stayed in the area, continued the family name and Catholic tradition. Other families have been parish members for many years."

In an era of lost services—schools, medical facilities, commerce—rural churches may have greater importance as rural community institutions. It is a challenge that denominational leaders have not overlooked and is the focus of much planning. It is incorrect, however, to assume that individual churches and the rural community are coterminous. This may occur if the community is composed of a single ethnic group of common religious affiliation, but such cases are rare at this stage of our history. Nor can cooperation among congregations in a community be assumed. While community churches in concert may claim to be arbiters of morality and performers of good works, they may not agree upon specifics and are in competition to attract and keep membership. Characteristically, church membership divides along lines of ethnicity, race, socioeconomic status, tradition, and family history of denominational identification. Such divisions are the basis for individual congregations' identification of membership domains within the community. Establishment of domains serves to reduce competition, but it also sets up barriers among congregations in the community.

Some congregations emphasize the forming of

religious communities and consciously with-draw, to a greater or lesser degree, from the secular community. One minister in the survey stressed that the church is a place of worship and not a social organization; on that basis, the church should have no community involve-ment. He pointed out that church funds should be used for only two purposes: (1) to preach and teach God's Word; and (2) to help qualified needy saints (fellow church members). Even those congregations that do not go so far in separation from the secular community tend to have characteristics of primary groups, being boundary conscious and internally directed; they represent particularistic views reinforced by common membership.

External relationships of congregations are not confined by the boundaries of the community. Most local congregations are affiliated with extra-local organizations, some of which extend worldwide. Congregations may contribute to charitable, health, and educational organiza-tions through their denominations, and also outside of such structures.

Support of Community Programs. Congregations may support a variety of community programs through sponsorship, financial contributions, and/or use of facilities. Support for a number of *types* of community programs was considered for 1967 and 1982 (comparable data were not available for 1952). The programs were: (1) youth organizations such as Boy Scouts, Girl Scouts, 4-H; (2) civil rights organizations and activities; (3) projects and programs to assist the disadvantaged; (4) temperance and prohibition organizations or activities; (5) general community programs—health clinics, bloodmobiles, programs for the elderly, educational programs. Youth organizations, assistance to the disadvantaged, and general community programs were those most often supported; virtually no sponsorship of civil rights or temperance programs was indicated. On the whole, support for the programs listed above was low, with less than half the congregations supporting any in 1982 (Table 5.1). Both size and type of congregation were factors in support of community groups. Large mainline churches were most likely, small nonmainline churches least likely, to sponsor or support community programs and organizations.

There appeared to be greater support of community programs in 1982 than there had been fifteen years earlier. The increase occurred for each category of congregation size and type (mainline/nonmainline). The magnitude of percentage changes was quite similar for both mainline and nonmainline congregations within the various size categories.

Intercongregational Relationships. Cooperation among congregations is indexed by the extent to which they engage in joint activities. Joint

97

Table 5.1

NUMBER OF COMMUNITY PROGRAMS* SUPPORTED
BY SIZE AND TYPE OF CONGREGATION, 1967, 1982

	Percentage Supporting One or More Programs	
Congregations	*1967*	*1982*
All Churches	23.8	41.8
Mainline	29.8	48.3
Nonmainline	9.1	28.0
Under 50 Members	7.7	25.3
Mainline	11.8	28.9
Nonmainline	2.7	21.1
50–99 Members	19.2	39.3
Mainline	22.3	46.0
Nonmainline	12.5	27.1
100 Members or More	42.8	59.8
Mainline	45.0	61.7
Nonmainline	25.0	50.0

*Youth Organizations; Civil Rights Organizations; Poverty Programs;
Prohibition or Temperance Organizations; General Community Programs

activities considered were: (1) evangelistic services, community-wide revivals, etc.; (2) worship services on special occasions—Easter,
Thanksgiving, Christmas; (3) vacation Bible
school; (4) pulpit exchanges; (5) CROP Sunday,
Rural Life Sunday, Rogation Sunday; (6) youth
programs.

It should be noted that there could have been other joint programs among congregations; the figures in Table 5.2 represent aggregations of the listed programs. In 1982, 53 percent of the congregations participated in at least one of the activities listed; worship services were the most common form of joint activity.

Participation in joint programs was positively related to size of congregation, but it should be noted that the two smaller size categories were quite similar, with the greater difference coming between them and the larger congregations. Overall and for each size category, joint programs were substantially greater for mainline than for nonmainline congregations.

For all congregations, only a small increase occurred from 1967 to 1982 in the proportion having at least one joint activity. Mainline and nonmainline congregations, however, moved in opposite directions: Mainline congregations were more likely to have joint activities in 1982 than in 1967; nonmainline congregations were less likely to have such activities. Furthermore, in all size categories, mainline congregations were more likely in 1982 than in 1967 to have at least one joint activity, while this was true for nonmainline congregations only in the largest size category.

Support of Charitable, Health, and Educational Organizations. Local religious groups reach beyond the boundaries of their communities to support charitable, health, and educational

Table 5.2

NUMBER OF JOINT ACTIVITIES* PARTICIPATED IN
BY SIZE AND TYPE OF CONGREGATION, 1967, 1982

| Congregations | *Percentage of Congregations Having One or More Joint Programs* | |
	1967	*1982*
All Churches	45.8	52.8
Mainline	49.6	61.3
Nonmainline	36.6	34.6
Under 50 Members	31.6	39.7
Mainline	30.8	48.1
Nonmainline	32.5	30.0
50–99 Members	44.7	50.0
Mainline	46.6	57.9
Nonmainline	40.4	35.4
100 Members or More	60.1	69.0
Mainline	62.3	72.1
Nonmainline	42.9	53.3

*Evangelistic Services; Worship Services; Vacation Bible School; Pulpit Exchange; CROP Sunday, Rural Life Sunday, Rogation Sunday; Youth Groups

organizations. In the year preceding 1982, 53 percent of the congregations contributed to homes for the aged; 33 percent, to hospitals; 55 percent, to children's homes; and 48 percent, to colleges. Most of the assistance was given through denominational channels to affiliated institutions, ranging from 81 percent for homes for the aged to 93 percent for colleges.

For 1982, size of congregation was positively related to contributions to charitable, health, and educational organizations, especially at the division between the largest category of churches and the two smaller categories (Table 5.3). Type of congregation (mainline/nonmainline) was strongly related to contributions. Eighty-one percent of mainline congregations, compared with 54 percent of nonmainline congregations, contributed to at least one charitable, health, or educational organization.

Several factors account for this difference: Nonmainline congregations are more likely to be directed inward, and therefore would not be as likely to support extra-congregational and, in most instances, extra-local organizations. Furthermore, the charitable, health, and educational organizations supported are often operated by or affiliated with religious denominations; as indicated earlier, most of the local support of these organizations moves through routine denominational channels. The mainline denominations tend to have more elaborate superstructures which include charitable, educational, and health organizations, and have more routinized ways to support them. Furthermore, a substantial number of nonmainline congregations claim no denominational affiliation.

Data are not available for local congregations' sponsorship of evangelizing activities, often associated with nonmainline churches.

Patterns of support for charitable, health, and educational organizations were similar at each time of observation—1952, 1967, and 1982. A small reduction was noted in the percentage of

Table 5.3

CONTRIBUTIONS TO CHARITABLE, HEALTH, AND EDUCATIONAL ORGANIZATIONS BY SIZE AND TYPE OF CONGREGATION, 1952, 1967, 1982

Educational, Health, and Charitable Organizations	*Percentage of Congregations Contributing to Organizations*		
	1952	*1967*	*1982*
Homes for the Elderly			
Total	54.3	57.0	53.0
Mainline	69.0	69.0	66.4
Nonmainline	13.4	27.6	24.4
Children's Homes or Orphanages			
Total	62.4	64.4	54.6
Mainline	74.7	74.3	66.1
Nonmainline	27.6	39.6	30.1
Hospitals			
Total	42.4	43.8	32.5
Mainline	56.1	55.4	45.0
Nonmainline	4.5	15.1	5.8
Colleges or Universities			
Total	——	57.0	47.9
Mainline	——	67.9	58.6
Nonmainline	——	29.9	25.0

congregations supporting the several types of organizations. The amount of reduction varied with the type of organization, with hospitals having the greatest; homes for the elderly, the smallest. These variations may be a result more of denominational than of local decision. There was some convergence in support of charitable, educational, and health organizations by mainline and nonmainline congregations. This came about from decreases in support by mainline congregations and increases by nonmainline. Still, it should be emphasized that the pattern of substantial difference between mainline and nonmainline congregations persisted over the entire period of observation.

Summary

Rural congregations relate to the community in a variety of ways. Some attempt to remove themselves from secular affairs; others claim identity with the secular community. Most congregations, however, fall somewhere between these extremes: They are occasional participants in community affairs, but devote most of their attention and resources to their own members.

Our data show differences of considerable magnitude between mainline and nonmainline congregations in participation in external activities. Thus, mainline churches were more likely to support community groups in one way or another; engage in joint programs with other local religious groups; and provide financial assistance to charitable, health, and educational organizations. It will be recalled from our earlier discussion that in some other characteristics, including facilities and complexity of internal organization, no clear differences existed between mainline and nonmainline congregations when size of congregation was taken into account. Furthermore, a convergence in these areas between mainline and nonmainline congregations occurred during the period of observation. In general, it is not in organizational complexity of local congregations or in material resources of congregations that we should look for distinction between mainline and nonmainline congregations, but in their approach to worship and their participation in the community.

While there is some indication that congregations were providing more support to certain community programs in 1982 than in 1967, the level was still quite low. Participation in intercongregational joint activities did not change much between 1967 and 1982; it is notable that nonmainline congregations, in aggregate, were less likely to participate in joint activities in 1982 than in 1967, while mainline congregations were more likely. This created greater divergence between the types of congregations in the latter than in the former year. In this respect, nonmainline congregations tended to maintain their exclusiveness in religious affairs.

When it comes to outreach programs that extend beyond the local area, such as those that support charitable, health, and educational organizations, there is no evidence of greater participation by congregations in 1982 than in 1952. It is quite clear that rural congregations are not being swept up in extra-local programs and activities. When they do participate, it is usually through the auspices of their mainline denominations. Rural congregations, it seems, remain what they were in the past—local institutional organizations of limited reach, with attention focused inward on congregational programs and activities.

VI

Who Ministers to Rural Congregations?

Who are the ministers of rural churches, and what do they do? A newspaper story usually gives the age, sex, location, and occupation of principal participants in a story, and from this information we supposedly learn the social status of the persons involved. While social *status* is the position an individual occupies in society, social *role* is a set of behavior patterns attached to a social status. Professions are powerful identifiers of status and prescribers of roles. They establish criteria for entrance, set standards of performance, develop codes of ethical practice, and provide collegial support. We expect persons in a particular profession to exhibit a resemblance to one another in training, activities, and evaluation criteria. Do the ministers of churches in rural Missouri represent a profession? If so, what are the criteria for membership?

In the first chapter we described the sampling procedures used in this study. Information on ministers is based on interviews with 341 ministers who served churches in the sample townships. There are several reasons for fewer ministers than churches in the sample: Some ministers served more than one church in the sample area; some churches were without a regular minister at the time of the interviews (temporary supply ministers were not interviewed); and some ministers were unavailable when interviews were conducted.

Demographic and Socioeconomic Background. The ministry in rural Missouri is overwhelmingly a male vocation; in 1982, 97 percent of the ministers were men, a figure that had not changed from 1952 (97%) or from 1967 (96%). Although a majority of the ministers were under 45 years of age in 1982, there appeared to be some aging when compared with the earlier surveys. By 1982, one in four ministers was 65 or older (Table 6.1).

Most ministers were from a local background in the sense of having been born in Missouri or an adjacent state (78%) and having grown up in a rural area. Until they were eighteen, 65 percent lived in places under 2,500 population, while 84 percent spent most of their youth in places under 50,000 population.

Background also included the occupational status of the ministers' families of origin. The fathers of about 7 percent of the ministers were also ministers; another 5 percent, other professionals. Eleven percent were owners or managers of businesses. Thus, about 22 percent of the fathers could be classified as professionals, or business owners and managers. If sales and clerical occupations are included in the white-collar category, then 30 percent of the fathers were in white-collar occupations. Another one-third were skilled and unskilled blue-collar workers; about one-third, farmers.

Table 6.1

CHARACTERISTICS AND BACKGROUNDS OF MINISTERS IN RURAL MISSOURI BY TYPE OF CONGREGATION, 1952, 1967, 1982

Ministers' Characteristics and Backgrounds	Percentage		
	1952	1967	1982
Age			
Under 35	28.0	26.0	13.0
35–44	22.0	24.0	42.0
45–64	34.0	37.0	20.0
65 and over	15.0	12.0	25.0
Native of Missouri or Adjacent State			
Total	79.1	84.3	78.2
Mainline	76.9	82.1	76.2
Nonmainline	85.9	88.0	82.9
Grew Up in Rural Area			
Total	78.0	72.3	65.2
Mainline	75.4	66.0	59.9
Nonmainline	85.9	85.5	76.5
Father in White-collar Occupation			
Total	22.0	19.9	29.9
Mainline	24.2	25.0	35.2
Nonmainline	15.3	9.9	18.1

Differences were small between ministers of mainline and nonmainline congregations, with respect to age structure and having been born in Missouri or adjacent states. However, non-mainline ministers were more likely to have spent most of their youth in a rural location; they also were less likely to have had fathers in white-collar occupations and more likely to have had fathers employed in farming.

The basic pattern of ministers' background characteristics had not changed much over the thirty-year period of observation. We have already noted some aging of ministers; little or no change was seen in place of birth. Although fewer had grown up in a rural area, still a substantial majority had rural backgrounds. A slight increase occurred in the percentage of ministers whose fathers were in white-collar occupations, and although Table 6.1 does not show the data, there was a substantial decrease in ministers from farm families. The increase in white-collar family backgrounds was greater for ministers of mainline denominations (Table 6.1). It is of interest to note that changes in place of residence while young and family background produce a closer match to the rural population of the state than if the changes had not occurred.

Careers of Rural Ministers. It is not entirely clear what point in a person's life can be marked as the beginning of a career. In professions such as medicine and law, standards of education as well as examinations are the basis for certification. Individual denominations may have such criteria, but for ministers in aggregate, educational criteria hardly apply. The range of education of rural Missouri ministers was striking—from less than high school to advanced degrees in theology and other disciplines. Thirty percent of the ministers had no formal educational experience beyond high school, with the possible exception of attendance at a Bible school. One-third had some academic college work, including those with a degree but no post-college work. Slightly over one-third had done post-college work.

Table 6.2

EDUCATION OF MINISTERS IN RURAL MISSOURI
BY TYPE OF CONGREGATION, 1952, 1967, 1982

Education of Ministers	Percentage		
	1952	1967	1982
Less than College			
Total	42.0	40.5	29.9
Mainline	28.8	20.0	17.0
Nonmainline	82.3	75.4	58.5
Some College Through Degree			
Total	29.9	26.7	33.7
Mainline	34.6	32.1	34.5
Nonmainline	15.3	17.6	32.1
Post-college			
Total	28.1	32.7	36.4
Mainline	36.6	47.9	48.5
Nonmainline	2.4	7.0	9.4

A great difference exists between the educational levels of mainline and nonmainline ministers. Fifty-eight percent of nonmainline ministers, compared with 17 percent of mainline ministers, had not attended college, with the possible exception of short-term Bible school attendance. On the other hand, 48 percent of mainline ministers, compared with 9 percent of nonmainline ministers, had postgraduate training, usually seminary training (Table 6.2). In separate questioning, it was found that ministers of nonmainline congregations were less likely than ministers of mainline congregations to report that both their denominations and congregations expected a minister to have at least a college education.

Although we may be surprised at the low level of education, that level has increased over the thirty-year period of observation, with the greater increase occurring in the last fifteen-year period. An apparent difference appeared in the patterns of change for ministers of both mainline and nonmainline congregations. From 1952 to 1982, a substantially greater percentage of both had attended college. The increase, however, was greater for nonmainline ministers, from 18 to 42 percent, than for mainline ministers, from 71 to 83 percent. The largest increase for nonmainline ministers was in the Some College category, while the largest increase for mainline ministers was in the Post-college category (Table 6.2).

Most of the ministers (58%) had entered the ministry by age thirty; 14 percent were forty or over. Twenty-six percent had served only one charge during their careers; 44 percent had served one or two charges. At the other extreme, 11 percent had served eight or more charges. The first church served by 78 percent of the ministers was in Missouri, and 64 percent of the ministers had not served a church outside the state; furthermore, a large majority (79%) had served churches only in nonmetropolitan communities. Eleven percent of the ministers had served their current charges for less than one year; 46 percent, for less than three years. Sixteen percent had tenure of ten years or more; 4 percent, of twenty-five years or more.

Ministers of nonmainline congregations, when compared with those of mainline congregations, had served fewer charges during their careers and, on the average, had longer tenure in the charges they were currently serving. The longer tenure and fewer moves of nonmainline ministers suggest that these people may be more closely and permanently tied to particular congregations. In some cases, it appeared as if minister and congregation formed an identity to the extent that a public distinction was not made between them.

Work of Rural Ministers. Ministers who had secular employment during the twelve months preceding the interview were classified as bivocational; 45 percent were so classified. The most common pattern was for bivocational ministers to work full-time in their secular occupations: Sixty-two percent worked 2,000 hours or more annually, which would be full-time employment; 18 percent worked under 1,000 hours. Secular work was quite evenly divided between white-collar jobs (professional, business owners and managers, sales and clerical) and blue-collar jobs (skilled and unskilled labor and farming).

There was some difference, but not a lot, in the percentage of mainline and nonmainline bivocational ministers—42 percent and 51 percent respectively. A decline in percentage of bivocational ministers had occurred since 1952, when 58 percent held secular occupations. The decline was greater for ministers serving nonmainline congregations than for their mainline counterparts; by 1982, the difference in the two types of ministers had been reduced from 24 percent to 9 percent. Still, a higher proportion of nonmainline ministers answered affirmatively when asked if their congregations and denomination representatives expected ministers to hold secular jobs.

Ministers' Household Incomes. Income of ministers' households for the year prior to the survey ranged from under $10,000 (17%) to over $30,000 (8%). The highest family income reported was $100,000, the principal source being a secular occupation. The median income of the households was $16,125. Church salary and compensation were the sources of at least half of the income in 49 percent of the households; a secular occupation of the minister accounted for half or more of the income in 33 percent. Other sources amounted to half or more of the household's income: pensions and social security (10%); spouse's and other family members' income (8%); and investments (1%).

Incomes of households of mainline and nonmainline ministers were similar, with some advantage for mainline ministers. Thus, 38 percent of households of mainline ministers, compared with 48 percent of households of nonmainline ministers, had incomes of under $15,000; 38 percent of mainline ministers, compared with 26 percent of nonmainline ministers, had incomes of $20,000 or more.

Ministers' Perceptions of the Present and Future. Ministers were asked several questions about their present situations and their perceptions of the future. About two-thirds—65 percent of mainline ministers and 73 percent of nonmainline ministers—felt that their present charges required maximum use of their time and skills.

A substantial proportion (43%), but not a majority, said that if they were to leave their present pastoral charge, they would prefer a larger one. Ministers of the two types of congregations did not differ appreciably on this preference—44 percent of mainline and 42 percent of nonmainline. Similarly, if ministers were to leave their "present location," 45 percent would like to live in a larger place. The difference between ministers of mainline and nonmainline congregations was greater on this, being 50 percent and 34 percent respectively.

Ministers were also asked to indicate two congregational sizes—the *minimum* size in which a satisfactory program could be carried out, and the *ideal* size. Ministers of nonmainline congregations were more likely than ministers of mainline congregations to report a smaller size for both the minimum and ideal size. To some degree, the difference in perceptions of mainline and nonmainline ministers reflects the tendency of nonmainline congregations to be smaller.

Finally, 40 percent of the ministers participated in community affairs by holding membership in at least one secular organization, such as a fraternal, service, patriotic, or special-interest group. Participation as civic officials was even lower; only 5 percent of the ministers held a local government office (e.g., school board member, town council member, county officer); 12 percent served on some kind of community committee. Differences between mainline and nonmainline ministers were apparent. Forty-six percent of mainline ministers, compared to 28 percent of nonmainline ministers, belonged to a secular organization. On the other hand, few differences were apparent between mainline and nonmainline in holding civic office and participating in community committees: Six percent of mainline and 4 percent of nonmainline ministers held civic office; 13 percent of mainline and 8 percent of nonmainline participated in community committees.

Roles of Ministers. Ministers of religious groups are present in almost every rural community. Their vocation is to provide leadership in spiritual and secular affairs to congregations of believers. Expectations for ministers, as they meet these obligations, are the basis for identifying their roles. Lawrence Hepple (1958: 210-12), in his earlier study of rural churches in Missouri, lists these roles. A minister is:

a symbol of religious ideals—a role-model based on religious values.

a prophet—an interpreter of God's will through sermons and teaching activities.

a priest—a practitioner of the religious group's liturgy and sacraments.

a student—a seeker of knowledge, especially through study and meditation on the Bible and other religious literature.

a pastor—one who cares for and ministers to the needs of a congregation.

an administrator—an executive who looks after the physical plant and financial affairs of the church.

a supervisor—a professional leader who trains and oversees the activities of lay leaders.

the church's representative in society—a spokesperson for the church in community and extra-local affairs.

116

Data are presented on the amount of time spent on activities, subsumed under the four roles which incorporate most of Hepple's list: the *ministerial-priestly role* (incorporating Hepple's prophet, priest, and student roles), the *pastoral role* (Hepple's pastor role), the *administrator role*, (incorporating Hepple's administrator and supervisor roles), and the *external activities role* (incorporating Hepple's symbol of religious ideals and church's representative in society roles). Samuel Blizzard (1956), among others, has discussed the potential for ministers' role conflict. On one level, role conflict may be due to allocation of time—for example, between sermon preparation and pastoral calling; on another level, it may involve differences in values—for example, whether to invoke business principles or charitable principles in use of resources. A role dilemma that faces some ministers is the difference in local and denominational expectations. Jeffrey Hadden (1969) discussed this problem with regard to ministers' participation in the civil rights movement, when denominational and local expectations were often at odds; more recently, some local congregations have objected to denominational support for international programs. Especially in their external activities role, ministers may be caught between these conflicting expectations.

A great deal of variation can be observed in the ways ministers relate to their congregations and communities. A few religious traditions do not acknowledge a professional clergy; and in a

117

manner compatible with the frontier experience, more place little social or spiritual distance between the minister and the lay people in the congregation.

"Preacher Bob," minister of a mainline congregation in a county seat (classified as a large village in our sample), leads an active congregation which recently built a new church on the outskirts of town. Although he is a seminary graduate and theologically sophisticated, he maintains little distance in dress or manner between himself and members of the community. On a summer day he wears a seed company hat and poplin work trousers; his transportation is a pickup truck; and he affects a country-style speech pattern. Although he says people know where he stands on social and moral issues, Preacher Bob tries not to antagonize his parishioners or other townspeople. Nor is he narrow in providing services, being willing to conduct funerals and weddings for nonmembers.

The Reverend Jones, in the same town and also a minister of a mainline church, does not blend so well into the community's life-style. For one thing, his denomination has recently assigned him to the three-congregation parish, and he expects to move in a few years. The Reverend Jones' manner is more formal than Preacher Bob's. A seminary graduate, he gives greater attention to the supervision of a sizable physical plant, to denominational matters, and to the ministerial-priestly role, particularly in the time he devotes to sermon preparation. He normally wears a coat and tie, which sets him apart from almost all the townspeople. He spends most of his day in his well-equipped church office and in making calls to hospital patients and church members in their homes.

These are only two composite descriptions of ministers' styles as they relate to congregations and communities. They are by no means extreme representations of a profession best described as composed of members of varied backgrounds, education, outlook, and practice.

Time Spent on Ministerial Activities. The amount of time spent on ministerial activities was derived by totaling the number of hours ministers reported spending on each of twelve ministerial activities. While these cover the normal activities, it is possible that some were excluded. At the same time, the procedure for adding separate categories may overestimate the time devoted; where very high total hours were recorded, this may be the case. However, it is also true that people in professions such as medicine and religion may regard virtually all their waking hours as being devoted to professional activities.

About 50 percent of the ministers spent less than 40 hours a week (including 15% who spent less than 20 hours) on the twelve ministerial activities. The other half of the ministers spent 40 or more hours a week (including 16% who spent 60 or more hours). In interpreting these figures, it should be pointed out that almost half the ministers were employed also in secular occupations.

Perhaps of more interest is the amount of time spent on specific activities. The twelve ministerial activities were grouped according to the following roles: *ministerial-priestly role*—sermon preparation, meditation and study, conducting services; *pastoral role*—visiting and calling on members, counseling with members; *administrator role*—administrative work, attending church committee meetings; *external activities role*—attendance at denominational, interdenominational, and community meetings.

In Table 6.3, the amount of time spent on each activity is shown. The category in which the median for ministers occurs is set in bold type. The greatest amount of time is devoted to ministerial-priestly role activities, with sermon preparation receiving the most time, closely followed by private meditation and study; the medians of both these activities come in the seven-hour category. The actual time spent conducting worship services, also a ministerial-priestly role activity, was lower, but still consumed more time than any other activity, except for visiting the sick.

Pastoral calling was an important role activity; 14 percent of the ministers spent at least nine hours a week visiting sick people. Calling on prospective members, "other" pastoral calling,

Table 6.3

HOURS A WEEK SPENT ON INDIVIDUAL MINISTERIAL ACTIVITIES, 1967, 1982

Activities	Hours Per Week									
	-1	1	2	3	4	5	6	7	8	9
	Percent of Ministers Spending									
Sermon Preparation	*This Number of Hours**									
1982	4	3	8	7	9	9	10**	2	9	40
1967	1	4	10	9	11	9	10	4	11	31
Private Meditation & Study										
1982	1	2	12	7	11	10	6	9	9	33
1967	1	3	10	10	10	9	9	6	6	34
Conducting Worship Services										
1982	1	11	16	25	19	8	10	2	3	5
1967	1	10	18	26	16	9	9	2	4	6
Visiting Sick Members										
1982	5	16	14	15	10	10	9	2	6	14
1967	7	13	21	12	12	5	6	3	4	17
Calling on Prospective Members										
1982	20	21	23	8	9	7	3	1	2	6
1967	20	22	17	12	10	5	3	2	4	5
Other Pastoral Calling										
1982	21	18	19	8	10	9	5	1	3	8
1967	23	15	15	9	7	6	5	1	4	13
Counseling Members w/Special Problems										
1982	14	27	18	11	11	5	4	2	2	6
1967	26	22	19	9	8	5	3	2	2	4
Administrative Work										
1982	30	14	9	7	6	6	2	3	4	19
1967	29	14	15	7	8	3	3	3	4	15
Attendance at Church Committee Meetings										
1982	38	32	14	5	4	2	2	—	—	1
1967	40	25	14	5	7	3	2	1	1	2
Attendance at Denominational Meetings										
1982	48	27	16	4	3	2	—	—	—	1
1967	42	27	15	4	6	3	2	—	1	—
Attendance at Interdenominational Meetings										
1982	81	15	3	—	1	—	—	—	—	—
1967	74	17	5	1	2	—	1	—	—	—
Attendance at Civic Club Meetings and Community Programs										
1982	71	17	7	2	1	1	—	—	—	—
1967	65	16	10	3	2	2	—	—	1	1

*Percentages rounded to nearest whole number.
Category in which the median number falls is set **bold.

and counseling were commonly engaged in, but with less time involvement.

Distribution of time in the administrative role is bimodal. Thirty percent of the ministers indicated they spent less than one hour per week on administration; at the other end of the distribution, 19 percent spent nine or more hours per week. This was the activity on which the highest percentage of ministers spent nine or more hours, with the exception of sermon preparation and meditation.

Participation in external activities was quite limited. Somewhat more time was spent on denominational meetings than those involving interdenominational, community, or civic affairs.

Ministers were asked, "If you were able to do your work exactly the way you would prefer, would you spend more, less, or the same amount of time in each of these (12) activities?" A substantial proportion of ministers would like to devote more time to each of the activities, but calling on prospective members was the activity to which most would like to devote more time. In general, the activities to which the ministers devote most time are those to which they *prefer* to devote more time—sermon preparation, meditation and study, and various pastoral activities that involve calling. Few ministers chose to devote less time to activities of the ministerial-priestly role or the pastoral role. The administrative and external roles did not fare as well. Administrative work was the activity on which the highest proportion of ministers (26%) would prefer to spend less time. "Attendance at church meetings," the other activity we identified as pertaining to the administrator role, was second to "administrative work" as the activity to which ministers would like to devote less time. Ministers did not devote much time to external role activities, and for the most part they would not choose to spend more; many could hardly spend less time, since they spent virtually none to begin with.

Similarities and differences appeared in the way ministers of mainline and nonmainline congregations allocated their time among the ministerial role activities. Differences were slight or nonexistent for private meditation and study, calling on prospective members, "other" pastoral calling, and counseling members with special problems. Ministers of mainline congregations were likely to devote more time to sermon preparation; visiting sick members; administrative work; attendance at church committee, denominational, interdenominational, and civic club meetings; and community programs. The only activity to which ministers of nonmainline congregations devoted more time than their mainline counterparts was in conducting services.

Patterns of hours worked by ministers in ministerial activities changed little from 1967 to 1982 (data are not available for 1952). At both times, mainline were more likely than nonmainline ministers to devote more hours per week to the twelve listed activities. Examination of the number of hours devoted per week, considered individually, also shows similar patterns for 1967 and 1982 (Table 6.3). The two years may be compared by determining the hour-category that contains the sample's median. For every activity except one (private meditation and study), the median number of hours fell in the same-hour category for both years; the exception was in an adjacent category.

Summary

Ministers of rural churches had a wide range of backgrounds, training, career paths, work patterns, and relationships to their congregations. They were almost always men, likely to have been born in Missouri or an adjacent state and reared in a nonmetropolitan area. Furthermore, rural ministers had not wandered far during their careers, which, for most, were confined within the state's borders.

In family background, number of locations, engagements in secular occupations, and allocation of time to role activities, there was sizable variation—for example, the variation in education. Most professions set minimum standards for certification. No such standards exist for clergy, and the educational range is from virtually no formal education to advanced degrees in theology and other fields. Rural ministers in this study were quite evenly divided among those who had no academic college training, those who had college work up to and including a baccalaureate degree, and those who had post-baccalaureate training.

The ministry differs from other professions, such as medicine and law, in another important way. The latter are almost always regarded as full-time vocations by their practitioners. In contrast, a substantial proportion of the ministers were employed in other occupations, and this was recognized as appropriate by many religious groups.

Time devoted to selected activities also showed variation among ministers. The ministerial-priestly role, involving preparation of sermons, meditation, study, and conducting worship services, received the most time allotment, followed by the pastoral role, which involved calling on and counseling members. Duties connected with administration and external relationships did not receive as much attention. Questioning revealed that most ministers would not choose to spend more time in administrative and external activities, but would like to spend more time in activities of the ministerial-priestly and pastoral roles.

Ministers of mainline and nonmainline congregations in aggregate were similar in some respects, different in others. They did not differ appreciably in place of birth or residence during their youth. There were some differences in family background, with ministers of mainline congregations likely to have fathers who were engaged in white-collar occupations.

Nonmainline ministers tended to have fewer moves in their careers and a longer tenure in their current churches; they appeared more likely to establish an identity between themselves and their church. Furthermore, they were somewhat more likely to have secular occupations, and their congregations were more likely to expect them to have such employment. Probably because of greater employment in secular occupations, ministers of nonmainline congregations spent somewhat fewer hours per week on the twelve selected role activities.

Among the role activities, ministers of mainline congregations were likely to spend more time on each of the administrative and external activities. There was no difference for three of the four pastoral role activities, but among the ministerial-priestly activities, ministers of mainline congregations were likely to devote more time to sermon preparation, while ministers of nonmainline congregations were likely to spend more time conducting services. There was no difference between ministers of the two types in time spent on private meditation and study. Differences in allocation of time were compatible with the common idea that ministers of mainline congregations were more concerned with organization, administration, and external relationships; whereas, ministers of nonmainline congregations tended to turn inward to the congregation, emphasizing the conducting of religious services.

Over the thirty years of observation, ministers

of rural churches in Missouri had aged some- what, they had become better educated, and they were not quite as likely to have secular employment. In spite of these observations, characteristics, in broad outline, were similar to those of 1952 and 1967. At all times of observation, the ministers were local in origin, ranged widely in education, and often depended on secular employment to support their families. The patterns of time devoted to twelve role-acti- vities were similar in 1967 and 1982.

At the beginning of this chapter, we ques- tioned whether the ministers of rural Missouri constituted a body of professionals. Using the criteria of professionals suggested, it is difficult to contend that they do. At the same time, many ministers in the study meet any reasonable criteria of professional status; many who do not would reject the professional model.

VII

Ministers' Theological Positions and Views on Selected Social and Moral Issues

Theology, the organized view of religious faith and practice, is central to a minister's vocation. Charles Glock and Rodney Stark, in a national sample of three thousand church members, examined the relationship between the members' theological positions and a wide range of moral and social issues. They commented, "Recently, we have rediscovered what should always have been obvious, that religious beliefs have important implications for the ways men evaluate, respond to, and act upon the world" (Glock & Stark, 1965:165-66). If theological position plays such a crucial role among church members, it should be at least as important for ministers, who are expected to articulate a particular theological position and to base their actions on it.

Ministers in the present study were asked to place themselves in one of three theological categories—liberal, conservative, or fundamentalist—without further explanation of those terms. It was possible to classify all responses except two in one of these categories, and three ministers did not respond to the question.

Ministers may have had different understandings of the categories and different reference points as the basis of response. A Southern Baptist minister, for example, who proclaims a liberal theological stance, may use only other ministers of his denomination as points of reference. Theological liberalism in the literature, however, is associated with modernist views, with an emphasis on social as well as spiritual needs. On an intellectual level, James Hunter (1983:33) says, "The new [liberal] theology (higher criticism and the like) signaled an acquiescence to the cognitive constraints of modern scientific rationalism—the desire to make sense of biblical literature in light of modern philosophical rationalism and the desire to make reasonable the Christian world view in the presence of hard seemingly contradictory evidence." Hunter characterizes fundamentalism as a reaction to modernism. Among the precepts of fundamentalism are "the infallibility of scripture, the deity and yet the historicity of Christ and his mission, personal salvation as a paramount concern for every person, and therefore the need for the evangelization of the world, and finally the bodily return of Christ" (Hunter 1983:34).

Background by Theological Position. Most of the ministers in the study considered themselves to be theologically conservative or fundamentalist. Fifteen percent said they were liberal; 52 percent, conservative; 33 percent, fundamentalist. There was no apparent difference in the age of ministers in the three theological positions (Table 7.1). Occupations of their fathers, however, showed differences: Liberal and conservative ministers had similar patterns, but they differed from fundamentalist ministers, who were more likely to have blue-collar and farmer backgrounds (Table 7.1). Differences of greater magnitude occurred in the educational level among ministers of the three positions. In general, liberal ministers had the highest level of education, followed in order by conservative and fundamentalist ministers. The educational patterns for liberal and conservative ministers were more alike than either was to fundamentalist ministers, but all theological categories contributed to the difference.

Situational Contexts by Theological Position. Churches served by fundamentalist ministers were more likely to be located in the open country, while congregations of liberal and conservative ministers were more likely to be located in large villages (places of 1,000 or more population).

Charges (all the congregations served by one minister) served by fundamentalist ministers were sharply smaller than those of liberal or conservative ministers, but the membership size of charges of the latter two types was similar. Thirty-eight percent of fundamentalist ministers, compared with 16 and 15 percent of liberal and conservative ministers respectively, served charges of under 50 members. At the other extreme, 26 percent of the liberal ministers and 21 percent of conservative ministers, compared with 3 percent of fundamentalist ministers, served charges of 300 or more members (Table 7.1).

Quite clearly, theologically liberal and conservative ministers were similar in background characteristics—age, family background, and education; and in situational context—size of place and membership of charges. Ministers of these two theological positions differed from fundamentalist ministers on all background and situational context factors, with the exception of age. Almost all (92%) liberal ministers served congregations of mainline churches, but note that most conservative ministers (81%) also served congregations of mainline denominations. Only fundamentalist ministers (40%) among the three theological positions, were less likely to serve mainline congregations.

Changes in Theological Positions. Ministers' reports of theological positions were available for 1967 and 1982, but the categories used in the two years were not entirely comparable. In 1967, ministers were asked which of these four theological positions best represented their views—liberal, neoorthodox, conservative, fundamentalist. In 1982, the neoorthodox category was not included. Dropping that category makes comparisons across the two periods imprecise. Those classified as neoorthodox in 1967 probably

Table 7.1

BACKGROUND AND SITUATIONAL CHARACTERISTICS OF MINISTERS IN RURAL MISSOURI BY THEOLOGICAL POSITION

Ministers' Characteristics		Theological Position				
	Liberal		Conservative		Fundamentalist	
	No.	Percent	No.	Percent	No.	Percent
Age of Minister						
Under 35	8	16.3	19	10.8	16	14.4
35–44	20	40.8	74	42.1	48	43.2
45–64	9	18.4	37	21.0	21	18.9
65 and over	12	24.5	46	26.1	26	23.4
Father's Occupation						
white-collar	18	38.3	60	34.7	20	18.3
blue-collar	16	34.0	52	30.1	45	41.3
farmer	13	27.7	61	35.3	44	40.4
Education of Minister						
less than college	6	12.2	28	15.9	66	59.5
some college	11	22.4	68	38.6	36	32.4
post-college	32	65.3	80	45.5	9	8.1
Size of Place of Congregation						
open country	12	25.0	57	32.4	56	50.5
200–999	15	31.2	62	35.2	29	26.1
1,000 and over	21	43.8	57	32.4	26	23.4
Total Membership of Charge						
under 50	8	16.3	26	14.8	42	38.2
50–99	5	10.2	41	23.3	37	33.6
100–179	10	20.4	34	19.3	22	20.0
180–299	13	26.5	38	21.6	6	5.5
300 or more	13	26.5	37	21.0	3	2.7

would have been divided between liberals and conservatives, had the neoorthodox choice not been available. This would have made the difference between 1967 and 1982 greater for liberals and less for conservatives than shown in Table 7.2. Thus there appears to be a rather substantial change away from a liberal theological position toward a conservative position, with a modest increase in the fundamentalist position.

Table 7.2

REPORTED THEOLOGICAL POSITIONS
OF MINISTERS, 1967, 1982

Theological Position	*Percentage of Ministers Reporting This Theological Position*	
	1967	*1982*
Liberal	21	15
Neoorthodox	9	—*
Conservative	37	52
Fundamentalist	31	33

*not available as a choice in 1982

Ministers' Views on Selected Social and Moral Issues. Ministers were asked to respond to a series of statements on current issues by indicating whether they supported or opposed them; the choice of neutrality was not offered, but it was recorded when volunteered.

Although the items were divided into social and moral issues (Table 7.3), there is a considerable amount of overlap between the two categories. The Equal Rights Amendment (ERA), women's right to choose abortion, racial integration, and capital punishment, while classified as social-issue items because they have entered the public arena of discussion and action, have strong moral content. Smoking and use of alcohol, while classified as moral issues because they involve rules of right and wrong imposed upon personal conduct, have become issues associated with health and accidents, thus subjects of public concern. Voluntary prayer in schools is considered a moral issue because of its obvious personal religious content.

A high level of consensus existed among rural ministers on the social issues; from 60 to 80 percent either supported or opposed the individual items (Table 7.3). The direction of the responses was conservative, in that most ministers opposed the ERA and women's right to choose abortion, and supported capital punishment and "workfare." However, a more liberal stance was indicated by the larger percentage of ministers who endorsed racial integration (the largest of any item) and limitation on nuclear arms. It is unclear whether the rejection of federal aid to education should be interpreted as a conservative or liberal stand.

The moral issues exhibiting the greatest consensus among respondents were sale of alcoholic beverages, social drinking, and smoking, all of which were opposed by more than 70 percent of ministers. Opposition to social dancing remains substantial, and there remain remnants of opposition to mixed swimming.

Ministers' Views by Type of Congregation. The first thing to be said about the pattern of responses to the questions on social and moral issues is that there was a definite difference between mainline and nonmainline ministers (Table 7.3). There were also other patterns of note. The division between ministers of mainline and nonmainline churches seemed more clear-cut on the moral-issue statements than on the social-issue statements. The direction of responses was consistent with expectations. Generally, nonmainline ministers took a more moralistic stand in regard to smoking, drinking, and social dancing. Mainline ministers were more supportive of a "liberal" stand on social issues—for example, opposition to capital punishment, but support of racial integration, limitations on nuclear arms, the Equal Rights Amendment, and women's right to choose abortion. The pattern of neutral responses is also of interest. Without exception, mainline ministers were more likely than nonmainline ministers to give a neutral response on moralistic statements, and in most cases the differences were substantial. On social-issue statements, however, mainline ministers were more likely to give a neutral response, although some exceptions were noted. In each case, the neutral response pattern may indicate relatively less intensity of concern—that is, less intensity

135

Table 7.3

MINISTERS' POSITION ON SELECTED SOCIAL AND MORAL ISSUES BY TYPE OF CONGREGATION

| Position on Issues | All Ministers | | Type of Congregation | | | |
| | | | Mainline | | Nonmainline | |
	No.	Percent	No.	Percent	No.	Percent
			Social Issues			
Federal Aid to Private Schools						
Support	57	16.8	38	16.2	19	18.1
Oppose	219	64.4	158	67.2	61	58.1
Neutral	64	18.8	39	16.6	25	23.8
Capital Punishment						
Support	208	61.4	136	58.1	72	68.6
Oppose	85	25.1	68	29.1	17	16.2
Neutral	46	13.6	30	12.8	16	15.2
Racial Integration						
Support	270	79.4	197	83.8	73	69.5
Oppose	24	7.1	13	5.5	11	10.5
Neutral	46	13.5	25	10.6	21	20.0
*Workfare**						
Support	257	75.6	169	71.9	88	83.8
Oppose	36	10.6	30	12.8	6	5.7
Neutral	47	13.8	36	15.3	11	10.5
Limitations on Nuclear Arms						
Support	202	59.2	154	65.5	48	45.7
Oppose	45	13.2	27	11.5	18	17.1
Neutral	93	27.5	54	23.0	39	37.1
ERA (Equal Rights Amendment)						
Support	66	19.4	60	25.5	6	5.7
Oppose	219	64.4	131	55.7	88	83.8
Neutral	55	16.2	44	18.7	11	10.5

				Moral Issues		
Right to Choose Abortion	Support	58	17.1	49	20.8	9	8.6
	Oppose	252	74.1	159	67.7	93	88.6
	Neutral	30	8.8	27	11.5	3	2.9
Sale of Alcoholic Beverages	Support	42	12.4	37	15.7	5	4.8
	Oppose	243	71.5	151	64.3	92	87.6
	Neutral	55	16.2	47	20.0	8	7.6
Smoking	Support	20	5.9	16	6.8	4	3.8
	Oppose	244	71.8	154	65.5	90	85.7
	Neutral	76	22.4	65	27.7	11	10.5
Social Dancing	Support	73	21.5	69	29.4	4	3.8
	Oppose	171	50.3	83	35.3	8	83.8
	Neutral	96	28.2	83	35.3	13	12.4
Mixed Swimming (of the Sexes)	Support	151	44.4	128	54.4	23	21.7
	Oppose	76	22.4	21	8.9	55	51.9
	Neutral	113	33.2	86	36.6	27	25.5
Social Drinking	Support	36	10.6	35	14.9	1	1.0
	Oppose	256	75.3	158	67.2	98	93.3
	Neutral	48	14.1	42	17.9	6	5.7
Voluntary Prayer in Schools	Support	231	67.9	146	62.1	85	81.0
	Oppose	67	19.7	56	23.8	11	10.5
	Neutral	42	12.4	33	14.0	9	8.6

*Welfare reform that requires recipients to work in public jobs.

Table 7.4

RESPONSES TO SELECTED SOCIAL AND MORAL ISSUES BY
MINISTERS IN RURAL MISSOURI BY TYPE OF CONGREGATION, 1967, 1982

Issues	All Ministers		Mainline		Nonmainline	
	1967 Percent	1982 Percent	1967 Percent	1982 Percent	1967 Percent	1982 Percent
Social Issues						
Capital Punishment						
Support	38.1	61.4	37.6	58.1	38.7	68.6
Oppose	42.5	25.1	46.9	29.1	35.2	16.2
Neutral	19.4	13.6	15.5	12.8	26.1	15.2
Racial Integration						
Support	77.2	79.4	86.6	83.8	61.3	69.5
Oppose	9.7	7.1	4.2	5.5	19.0	10.5
Neutral	13.1	13.5	9.2	10.6	19.7	20.0

Moral Issues

Smoking						
Support	11.8	5.9	15.9	6.8	4.9	3.8
Oppose	65.1	71.8	59.8	65.5	73.9	85.7
Neutral	23.1	22.4	24.3	27.7	21.1	10.5
Social Dancing						
Support	24.1	21.5	35.1	29.4	5.6	3.8
Oppose	61.7	50.3	47.3	35.3	85.9	83.8
Neutral	14.2	28.2	17.6	35.3	8.5	12.4
Mixed Swimming						
Support	45.5	44.3	56.9	54.4	26.2	21.7
Oppose	25.8	22.3	12.6	8.9	48.2	51.9
Neutral	28.7	33.1	30.5	36.6	25.5	26.5
Social Drinking						
Support	8.7	10.6	12.6	14.9	2.1	1.0
Oppose	84.0	75.3	78.2	67.2	93.7	93.3
Neutral	7.3	14.1	9.2	17.9	4.2	5.7
Sale of Alcohol						
Support	9.4	12.4	13.3	15.7	2.8	4.8
Oppose	80.1	71.5	73.3	64.3	91.5	87.6
Neutral	10.5	16.2	13.3	20.0	5.6	7.6

of concern of nonmainline ministers for social issues and of mainline ministers for moralistic issues.

Changes in Ministers' Views. Particular social issues in the forefront of public attention at one time may not be important at another time. For example, in 1967 the Vietnam war was a matter of public concern, and a survey question about it was appropriate; it was not a public concern at the time of the 1982 survey. On the other hand, a question about the Equal Rights Amendment was meaningful in 1982, but not in 1967. Only two common social-issue items were asked in both 1967 and 1982, but several comparable moral-issue items were asked at both times (Table 7.4).

The largest shift in ministers' positions had to do with capital punishment, for which there was more support in 1982 than in 1967. Ministers of both mainline and nonmainline congregations showed greater support for capital punishment, with ministers of nonmainline congregations registering the greater change. Since capital punishment was debated as a political issue during this period, positions on it probably were more crystallized at the later date. It may also reflect a more conservative stand by clergy. Racial integration, the second social issue, was supported at about the same levels in 1967 and 1982, with little change among ministers of mainline congregations and a relatively small increase for ministers of nonmainline congregations.

On moral issues, there was little change among ministers of nonmainline congregations. The vast majority was opposed to sale of alcoholic beverages and social drinking at both times, and only a slightly smaller percentage was opposed to smoking and social dancing at the later time. Ministers of mainline congregations took somewhat less moralistic stands. Between 1967 and 1982 a slight decrease appeared in the percentage of ministers opposed to the sale of alcoholic beverages, social dancing, social drinking, and mixed swimming (Table 7.4). The change, for the most part, was not from opposition to support, but to a neutral stand. The change in smoking percentages, however, was toward greater opposition. This is understandable because smoking had become more of a health-social issue. In summary, there appears to be a slight erosion of opposition among ministers of mainline congregations toward selected practices that could be judged on a moralistic basis, while ministers of nonmainline congregations held firm.

Summary

Ministers, as part of their vocation, are expected to take theological positions and translate them into views about social and moral issues. In this chapter we have related ministers' self-reported theological positions to their backgrounds, to their situational contexts, and to the type of congregation served (mainline or nonmainline). We have also examined expressions of support and opposition to selected social and moral issues.

A majority of ministers reported that they were theologically conservative or fundamentalist. Ministers who espoused liberal and conservative theology were quite similar in background, measured by father's occupation and ministers' level of education; and in situational context, measured by location and size of congregation. But they were quite different from fundamentalist ministers on all these factors.

From the tabulation of ministers serving mainline and nonmainline churches, it is clear that almost all liberal ministers served mainline churches, whereas fundamentalist ministers were likely to serve nonmainline churches.

A rather high level of consensus prevailed among ministers on many social and moral issues. A large majority (60% or more) opposed ERA and women's right to choose abortion, but supported capital punishment, workfare, and racial integration. A large majority also opposed the sale of alcoholic beverages, smoking, and social drinking. The expected relationship existed between type of congregation (mainline or nonmainline) served by ministers and their responses to social and moral issues.

Because of differences in questioning in the 1967 and 1982 surveys, evidence of changes in theological position of ministers was imprecise; however, there appeared to be some shift away from the liberal position toward the conservative. The percentage of fundamentalist ministers was virtually unchanged. Aside from a higher incidence of support for capital punishment, there was not much change in response patterns on social and moral issues. Overall, we did not detect the massive shifts toward fundamentalism and conservatism that are sometimes thought of as being characteristic of contemporary U.S. religion. Religious conservatism, fundamentalism, and related themes are clearly important elements among rural churches and their ministers. This, however, is no revolution and there has not been much change.

VIII

Summary and Interpretation

We can make few precise statements about the programs and characteristics of rural churches that would apply to all congregations in the survey, since congregations vary in size, organization, and programs, and in relationship toward the community and the wider society. We can, however, indicate some prominent characteristics of rural churches and their ministers, and attempt to sharpen our understanding of such churches through interpretation.

Churches of Rural Missouri. The rural churches in the survey had simple facilities, internal organization, and programs. Buildings were modest, although most contained kitchen and dining facilities. A majority of the congregations depended heavily on volunteer labor for maintenance of the building and grounds and for simple renovations; a bare majority of the congregations expected to hire workers for major building and repair work. Generally speaking, rural churches existed on limited economic resources. Size of congregation was closely related to the material goods and income

144

of the congregation; when size of congregation was controlled, little difference in facilities or income existed between mainline and nonmainline congregations.

Most congregations held weekly worship services and conducted weekly Sunday schools; Sunday evening services, midweek services, and annual revival services were quite common, but occurred more often in nonmainline than in mainline congregations. The presence of various kinds of religious services was affected less by size of congregation in nonmainline than in mainline congregations; most nonmainline congregations of all sizes held these services, while large mainline congregations were more likely to hold them than were small mainline congregations.

The internal organization of most congregations, as indicated by the types and number of suborganizations, also was quite simple. While most of the congregations had Sunday schools and a small majority had a women's organization, the proportion fell below one-half for choirs, separate study groups, and youth organizations. Only a few congregations had such suborganizations as a men's group, and young-adults' group, or an older-adults' group. Size of congregation was closely related to whether or not suborganizations were present, but there was little difference between mainline and nonmainline congregations when size of congregation was controlled.

Organizational simplicity extended to formalization of activities. Two-thirds of the congregations did not have a written contract with their minister, nor was there much formalization in raising money through every-member canvasses and pledges. The simplicity of the administrative component is indicated by the report of 44 percent of the ministers that they spent no more than one hour a week on administrative tasks.

In general, rural congregations directed their attention to programs of worship, instruction, and fellowship for their own members. They were variably involved in community activities; in support of health, education, and charitable agencies; and in participation with other local congregations in joint programs and activities. Size of congregations made a difference in whether or not congregations participated in these extra-congregational programs and activities, and mainline congregations were more likely than nonmainline congregations to participate. More pointedly, it was on external rather than internal relationships that mainline congregations and nonmainline congregations seemed to be most organizationally distinct. Such differences seem consistent with our understanding that mainline churches are more in the mainstream, while nonmainline churches tend to separate themselves in various ways from the secular community.

Ministers of Rural Missouri. As was the case with the organization, programs, and activities of churches, there were great differences in the background, education, careers, work patterns, and opinions of ministers who serve rural churches. To a high degree, however, the ministers reflected the background of the members of their congregations: They were likely to be native Missourians, reared in rural communities. Furthermore, most had grown up in the homes of farmers or blue-collar workers. The range of education was astonishing—from grade school to full theological training in some of the nation's finest schools. College and post-college training were more common for ministers serving mainline than for those serving non-mainline congregations.

The tenure of ministers in their churches varied; nonmainline ministers tended to have longer tenure and were more likely to be symbolically identified with their congregations. Ministers often had secular employment, and this substantially reduced a congregation's economic responsibility for support of a minister.

The ministers of rural churches spent most of their time on the ministerial-priestly role activities of sermon preparation, study and meditation, conducting services, and the pastoral-role activities of visiting and calling on members; less time on administrator-role duties; and little on external role activities involving denominational, interdenominational, and community participation. Nonmainline ministers, compared with mainline ministers, were likely to devote more time to conducting services and less to administration.

The self-reported theological position of most ministers was either conservative or fundamentalist. Liberal and conservative ministers were quite similar in background, education, and situational context (size of place where their churches were located and membership of their congregations), but both were quite different from fundamentalist ministers on these factors. A pattern showed that ministers of nonmainline denominations were likely to report a fundamentalist theological position, with ministers of mainline denominations likely to report a conservative or liberal position. Extremely few liberal ministers served nonmainline congregations.

Ministers' responses to social and moral issues showed a conservative stance. They expressed strong opposition to abortion, the ERA, federal aid for private schools, sale of alcoholic beverages, smoking, and social drinking. There was strong support for capital punishment, voluntary prayer in school, and racial integration. The type of congregation a minister served (mainline or nonmainline) was related, as expected, to the minister's views on social and moral issues.

Changes in Churches and Ministers. A major finding of this study is the stability in the number of churches in rural Missouri when charted over a thirty-year period. Only 6 percent fewer congregations existed in 1982 than in 1952. Although the numbers did not change greatly over the period, there was greater volatility than the totals convey. During that period, 130 congregations went out of existence, countered by 98 additions. There was a noticeable shift of church locations from the open country to larger villages, resulting from greater losses and fewer replacements in the open-country category. There was also a slight proportional increase in the congregations with more than one hundred members. Perhaps the most notable change was the relative increase in nonmainline congregations, when compared with mainline congregations. The gain in nonmainline congregations was especially strong in the Ozarks, but occurred also in the Commercial Agricultural Area. We should emphasize that the changes cited were quite gradual over the thirty-year period and tended to be similar for each of the fifteen-year periods observed. These kinds of changes, for the most part, seem to be compatible with the more general changes in rural society.

Observations of change included not only the numbers of congregations, but their facilities, internal organization, program, and external relationships. As with stability in numbers of congregations, we must be impressed with the stability of the internal organization and programs of rural churches, but some changes have occurred. There appears to be a general rise in their level of living. Higher percentages of congregations owned selected material items in

1982 than was true fifteen or thirty years earlier. Nonmainline congregations increased material possessions more than did mainline congregations, so at the end of the thirty years, the two types were more alike than at the beginning. There also was an increase in the proportion of congregations that held Sunday worship services every week. This too might be regarded as an increase in "level of living."

Perhaps somewhat surprising, the traditional congregation-wide Sunday evening services, midweek services, and annual revivals continued to be widely conducted. Their durability can be attributed to being part of the "model programs" of many of the nonmainline and Southern Baptist congregations.

A pervasive change in the programs and internal organization of congregations—a tendency toward convergence of mainline and nonmainline congregations—occurred not only in facilities, but also in internal organization. Suborganization convergence came about mainly from changes in nonmainline congregations as they became more complex. Over the period of observation, the differences between mainline and nonmainline congregations in facilities, internal organization, and activities, which had been so pronounced in 1952, had diminished substantially. Furthermore, when size of congregation was taken into account, there was little difference between mainline and nonmainline congregations in many of the above characteristics.

The picture is somewhat different when consideration is given to programs and activities that extend beyond the congregations to the community and wider society. There, the differences between mainline and nonmainline congregations have not shown the same degree of convergence and, in some instances, show divergence. It appears that congregations supported more community programs in 1982 than they had in 1967, although the level of support was low at both times. The difference in favor of mainline congregations was similar for both survey years. The percentage of congregations contributing to educational and service organizations (homes for the elderly, children's homes, hospitals, colleges), in most cases was smaller in 1982 than in 1952. The considerable difference between mainline and nonmainline congregations tended to persist for the different survey years. Finally, from 1967 to 1982, mainline and nonmainline congregations appeared to have moved in opposite directions in their participation in joint activities with other congregations in the community.

Our general observation is that the internal organization and activities of mainline and nonmainline congregations were more similar in 1982 than they had been in 1952. This convergence, however, did not carry over, at least to the same extent, into external relationships with the community, with local congregations, or with the wider society.

In many respects, the characteristics of ministers in rural Missouri in 1982 were much like those in 1952 and 1967. Ministers were very much a part of their communities in background and beliefs. In the most recent survey, they were somewhat more likely to have grown up in white-collar families, but this was also more the character of rural employment at the later time. There was also an increase in the level of education, with ministers of nonmainline congregations more likely to have some college education, and ministers of mainline congregations more likely to have post-college work, than was true in 1952. The increases were gradual, and even in 1982, educational levels were extraordinarily varied.

In 1982, a fairly large percentage of the ministers continued to have a secular occupation, although the figure was somewhat lower than in the previous survey years. The patterns of hours worked and the activities to which ministers devoted time remained remarkably similar for 1967 and 1982 (data were not available for 1952).

There appeared to be a movement among ministers from a liberal toward a more conservative theological stance, but the percentage of ministers reporting fundamentalist theology was similar for 1967 and 1982. There were no major shifts between 1967 and 1982, however, in ministers' opinions on social and moral issues, with the exception of greater support for capital punishment. Despite the attention that conservative religion is receiving on the national level, it appears there has been no revolution and only modest change in opinions of already conservative/fundamentalist rural ministers.

Interpretation of Characteristics and Changes. Throughout the reporting and discussion of this study, we have attempted to place churches and ministers in the context of rural society and the changes in rural society. Our interpretation makes these contextual relationships more explicit.

There is abundant evidence that rural society underwent many changes in the thirty-year period covered by the surveys of rural churches in Missouri. During the first two decades of that period, the population in rural areas declined, but the trend reversed, and the last decade showed an increase. The decline and growth were variable by section of the state and from township to township.

Other changes of equal or greater consequence also occurred. Trade centers evolved in relationship to their hinterlands and to other centers. Some centers became larger and served a larger trade area, while others declined as service centers to survive as residences for people who are retired or commute to other places for employment. This concentration affected not only commercial establishments, but other institutions, especially schools and health services. Open-country schools were virtually eliminated, and high schools were consolidated into larger units at fewer locations; physicians abandoned the smallest towns for places with hospital facilities.

A third general change in rural Missouri involved employment, which, since 1950, has been dramatic, consisting of a sharp decrease in the proportion of the labor force engaged in agriculture and a sharp increase in women in the labor force. Comparisons of population and our field observations confirm that our sample townships conform closely to these statewide changes.

Broadly, we can characterize these changes as an urbanization of rural society, which results in greater internal mobility and diversity of population and less isolation from organizations of the larger society. We can observe that such institutions as schools, commercial firms, and health services have responded in ways compatible with urbanization. How do we interpret the churches' responses to these influences?

We are not entirely disappointed in our attempt to relate changes in rural congregations to the urbanization of rural society. We note that the number of congregations was more likely to increase in townships that were growing in population than in those losing population; that diversification of population opened up opportunities for growth of nonmainline congregations; and that losses of congregations in the open country and gains in larger villages were compatible in direction, if not in detail, with changes in other service organizations.

However, how do we explain a different set of observations which relate to the survival of rural churches and their organizational stability in both internal and external programs? We suggest that rural churches have, to some degree, insulated themselves from the most direct influences of the larger society. As the basis for direct influences of systems of the larger society on local units, crucial relationships are maintained. In developing these relationships, local units may become specialized and dependent upon centralized units.

To apply this reasoning to local churches, we find that as local congregations become more dependent on denominational centers for program, organizational models, and leadership (clergy), they also are more subject to the influences of those centers. Then expectations and requirements exist for certain levels of performance, and local congregations may be established or closed as parts of overall denominational plans. Merging congregations and the formation of multicongregation parishes are often products of extra-local decisions. Our most general conclusion is that rural churches have, to some degree, avoided these interdependencies and therefore are not highly sensitive to centralized influences of urbanized society. In a general way, the congregations' self-sufficiency tends to insulate them from the direct effects of the bureaucracies of the larger society.

The organizational structure of rural congregations contributes to their insulation. A large proportion of the rural churches retains congregational governance, and congregations may react negatively to efforts to centralize their activities. Such reactions have a long history, including the Baptist antimissionary movement (Sweet, 1950), and the more recent defections of congregations to independent status when the Christian Church (Disciples of Christ) moved toward greater centralization. Furthermore, decisions by a denomination to close a church does not necessarily result in a congregation's demise, since it may survive as an independent congregation or under different auspices.

The programs of rural churches may guard them from influences of the larger society. Programs emphasize worship services and are turned inward toward members of the congregation, in Sunday schools, Bible studies, revivals, and traditional midweek and Sunday evening services. The nearly universal Sunday school is an example of the self-sufficient character of local church programs; they tend to be lay people's activities, and greater continuity may be found in the Sunday school than in any other part of a congregation's program.

Insulation from the wider society is fostered also by the simplicity of the churches' internal organization. Simple organization places relatively light organizational demands on congregations, with little attention needed for administration of programs.

There is abundant evidence from the survey that rural congregations had limited participation in the secular affairs of the community or the wider society. This was also true for activities in which ministers might engage.

The fact of low financial needs of rural churches is also a statement of low financial obligations of members. The simple buildings and minimum expenses for professional leaders exempt rural churches, to a large degree, from demands of the market. Most rural congregations have not taken the step of rationalizing finances to the point of pledged commitments from members. The self-sufficient church, as well as the self-sufficient farmer, is not affected much one way or another by the marketplace. At the present time, in the case of farmers, it is clear that economic self-sufficiency contributes to survival of the enterprise; the case for the self-sufficient church is parallel.

The characteristics and relationships of ministers to community and congregation are additional factors that tend to exempt congregations from influences of the larger society. Vidich and Bensman (1958) indicated in their study of a small New York community that the clergy were a link between the local community and the wider society; in particular, the clergy introduced the thoughtways of the larger society to the local community. We found, however, that ministers of rural Missouri churches closely reflect the background and the thoughtways of their communities. Furthermore, many rural ministers do not carry the educational credentials often associated with professional status. Thus local congregations and their ministers are released from some of the constraints of a standard-setting professional system. The clergy also contribute to the exemption of local congregations from economic demands of the larger society by gaining financial support from secular occupations. This too is a traditional mode of behavior, an extension of the unpaid farmer-preacher who served a frontier church.

Finally, our original expectation was that the rural churches would be uniformly affected by the influences of the larger society; this does not seem to be true. Some congregations were in the crucial relationship with elements of the larger society alluded to earlier; others were not. This is seen most clearly in the differential experiences of mainline and nonmainline congregations in maintaining congregations over the thirty-year period of observation.

The Rural Church as a Primary Group

We have come to regard rural churches as primary groups. In this respect, rural schools and rural churches, although having much in common in their beginnings, have taken sharply divergent paths. The local school has been incorporated into a complex educational system, with guidelines, resource allocations, and control emanating from bureaucracies at the state and national levels. From neighborhood institutions, schools have become local components of specialized organizational systems, removed to some extent from direct community control through professionalization of staff, standardization of curriculum, extra-local evaluation of programs, and major state and national financing. Consolidation of schools (often to meet state requirements) has effectively eliminated neighborhood country schools and changed the location patterns of primary and secondary attendance units. Opposition to the closing of open-country schools often was posed in terms of loss of neighborhood identity; to the closing of small high schools, as the loss of community. Because the purpose of a school was narrowly defined and did not include the maintenance of neighborhoods and communities, these arguments were to no avail; the local units had lost control.

Rural churches, for the most part, have not followed the same course. They have remained locally oriented and dependent. Specialization, in the form of organizational elaboration and professional leadership, has been resisted and remains minimal; congregational control continues, in fact and in spirit; traditional programs persist; and moral precepts correspond to those of the locality. The buffer that local congregations have raised to denominational and other extra-local influences is in the form of primary group relationships.

Primary groups, in the sociological jargon, are small face-to-face groups whose members relate to one another in a whole range of settings and are bonded by affective relationships—love and

159

loyalty. The family is the prototype primary group; other common examples are peer groups (friendship cliques) and neighborhoods. Primary groups are based upon members' similarities in social class, ethnicity, race, and other factors. Different congregations within the same community can accommodate the particularism upon which primary groups are based. The nature of primary groups, however, tends to constrain wide-ranging relationships and turn them inward toward members of the group. As the rural population becomes more diverse economically and in background, we might expect greater diversity of religious groups; this expectation is compatible with increases in nonmainline congregations. As challengers to mainline congregations, nonmainline congregations may exhibit intense primary-group characteristics.

Primary groups thrive on tradition and group memory; they attend to the needs of their members; they define morality in personal terms within the precepts of the group and encourage conformity through informal means of control such as gossip and ostracism. In primary groups, bonding offers support for those within the group in times of crisis. The dark side of such intense relationships can lead to sharp and personalized disagreements within the group and tend to separate groups within the community. The autonomous congregations of frontier tradition are rife with such splintering.

Primary groups, furthermore, are weak in the areas of program development, record keeping, and action on wider social issues of the community and beyond. They are, in a word, frustrating to denominational officials who have the responsibility for organization and program, but limited authority (Harrison, 1959).

Wade Roof (1976:197), a sociologist of religion, comments that in the U.S., church religion "is increasingly restricted to smaller 'subworlds' of social experience." He contends that the subworlds "are associated more with private than with public sectors of life; and structures such as the family, ethnic group or some other limited social sphere play a crucial part in sustaining personal religious loyalties." In this sense, rural churches in Missouri are in conformity with those on the national scene. It also suggests to us that rural churches may not be effective agents for community integration, but are agents of particularism within the community.

In general, the study of the rural church informs us of the organizational dynamics of rural society and suggests qualifications to the concept that elements of the larger society act unrestrictedly on local organizations. Generally, however, little attention has been given to the qualities of organizations that mitigate the influences of the larger society on organization, programs, and activities of particular local groups.

The Rural Church in the Community

Maintenance of communities is a major challenge in rural areas. Our image of a viable rural community is one that preserves a degree of local control and responds to needs of community members, while relating effectively to the institutions of the larger society. Rural communities desperately need local organizations that can serve local needs and, at the same time, contend with issues and constraints of the larger society. The very process of urbanization of rural society presents a dilemma. Marked by extensive consolidation and centralization, urbanization leaves many local communities without essential institutional organizations such as schools, medical facilities, and retail businesses. A defense against consolidation and centralization (and thereby loss of local services) is a disengagement from the national arena through isolation and insularity. The costs of such a strategy, however, are severe; they include surrender of power in extra-local affairs.

Churches occupy a unique position in the community because they combine a degree of local control with a connection to extra-local organizations, represented by denominations. The need for such institutions is great. We have observed the rather remarkable survival qualities of rural churches and have emphasized that their survival depends upon their relatively low demands on economic resources. Enmeshed in local cultures, rural churches reinforce local norms within primary-group settings. This places them on the side of insulation from the imperatives of the larger society.

But we also have learned from the research that rural churches do not escape the effects of urbanization. Centralization is clearly seen in the losses of open-country congregations and consolidation of mainline congregations; congregations have responded as expected to population gains and losses; and diversification of population has nurtured nonmainline congregations.

Tensions between localism and extra-localism are handled differently by different congregations. From an overall view of rural churches, we gain appreciation of variation in size, history, internal organization, leadership, community relationships, and relationships with extra-local religious bodies. *The* rural church, as it turns out, is a myth—there are many rural churches.

The idea of the autonomous rural church can be overemphasized. While rural churches are highly dependent upon their localities for the resources of money and participants, it is clear that most of them are supported in some ways by denominational bodies. Support may be direct financial assistance, but it is more likely to be in the form of consultation, preparation and distribution of literature, training of ministers and other church workers, recruiting of ministers, and planning of activities. Denominational authority also legitimates local practices as proper and certifies ministers as qualified.

Congregation/denomination relationships are analogous to franchise relationships in business. The denomination depends on a flow of resources from local congregations—especially money—but also for personnel; people are prepared through socialization in local churches for training and service in denominational programs such as seminaries, colleges, service agencies, and missionary work. Denominational affiliation benefits local congregations in ways indicated above, plus the potential of gaining transfer members. When Methodist Mary James, upon retirement, moves from Chicago to the Ozarks, the local Methodist church gains a member. More generally, to the benefit of the local franchise, denominations advertise their presence in many ways, from logos to television programs. The relationship between congregations and denominations is primarily an exchange of resources—money and socialized personnel contributed by local congregations for legitimacy, and organizational and theological direction by the denomination. In the exchange, however, small congregations are low producers of resources and may be poor receivers of denominational counsel.

Wide differences exist in the tightness of coupling between congregations and denominations. Denominational exchange is available, to some extent, for most rural congregations. Some denominations exercise hierarchical authority, but even in denominations with congregational polities, such as Baptists, central control is extensive. Informants for Churches of Christ, which were represented in the study by a substantial number of congregations, resolutely claimed that they are independent of any denomination, and, in fact, there is no organizational superstructure. However, Churches of Christ have common sources of literature, maintain common and distinct practices, and advertise their presence by a common name. The same can be said for independent Baptist and Christian churches. At the very extreme of separation from larger church bodies are the congregations of entrepreneurial ministries, but their number is not large.

Variation occurs in the ways congregations define and carry out their missions. We have tried to capture broad differences by using the mainline/nonmainline distinction. These *types* conform to the "church"/"sect" typology. In the classical literature (Troeltsch 1960; Pope 1942), the concepts *sect* and *church* identify two *types* of religious groups. The *sect* has an inward-turning orientation which stresses religious services and immediacy of religious experience. It involves close emotional ties between participants. Martin Marty (1960) observed that sects offer simplification in an overly complex society. The *church*, by contrast, is oriented more toward the external environment (community and larger society), stresses more formal and organized practice, and is engaged with the secular world rather than withdrawn from it.

165

Even though the mainline/nonmainline categories are very broad, they do show consistent differences in the present study. Congregations are subject to contradictory pressures. On the one hand, the models of denominations may push congregations to elaborate programs, seek more professionalized ministers, develop more complex organizational structures, and become more accountable to the denominational bureaucracies. Yet on the other hand, rural churches are faced with diminishing local resources. When population declined in many rural areas—it grew older in most—and much of the state's rural area fell into economic crisis, mainline and nonmainline congregations tended to respond differently. Mainline congregations appear to be caught in the middle of both trends. So among them, we observe a decline in number of congregations, with a particularly large reduction in the open country; greater professionalization of clergy; and increased frequency of worship services. By contrast, nonmainline congregations actually have increased in number through a painful process of multiple losses and additions. They too have elaborated programs but, in aggregate, remain less organizationally developed and smaller in size. Their clergy are less professionalized by the criterion of education, devote less time to administrative tasks, and are more likely to take a fundamentalist theological position. Non-mainline congregations are less likely to participate in community activities, to hold joint activities with other local congregations, or to support extra-local charitable, health, or educational agencies.

One explanation for the difference in the aggregate survival experience of mainline and nonmainline congregations is the cost of starting and maintaining their respective programs. Mainline congregations generally operate from a model that requires more resources, and they are more likely to be subject to denominational program formulas. Therefore, when faced with declining local resources, they adjust by moving away from the most marginal settings, and concentrate resources in more resource-adequate locations. The nonmainline congregations, on the other hand, maintain a less expensive model. They survive somewhat better in resource-poor environments, where they put forward a minimal program that does not extend beyond the fellowship group.

A result of these trends is a changed balance between mainline and nonmainline congregations. These changes, we think, have an impact on the viability of rural communities. For while the number of congregations remains relatively stable, we see a decline in the capacity of local congregations to link their members to the national level and combat the tendencies toward insulation from the mainstream. This contributes to a further peripheralization of rural communities. Also, the nonmainline congregations, with a high rate of deaths and births, are more volatile than mainline congregations. This quality lends additional instability to fragile rural communities beset by economic crisis.

For ministers and church leaders entering or already working in the rural field, there are challenges aplenty. For rural communities, as well as for denominations and individual congregations, the stakes are high. It would be presumptuous, however, to detail a model agenda for rural churches. A single model would not be appropriate for all congregations or for all situations. We think, however, that practitioners should enter the rural church field as informed as possible about rural society and the role of the church in it. Part of that understanding involves the changes that have occurred in rural society, and the potential of rural churches and their leaders in shaping the rural community.

The survival of rural congregations in an urbanizing rural society stands out. Our sociological sense tells us that programs should build upon the churches' strength as fellowship groups enmeshed in local cultures. Such groups have the ability to support their members in stressful situations, now common in rural areas. The potential, though, may be frustrated by congregational exclusiveness. The challenge is to extend support more widely and to become an active participant in community affairs. The promise for dealing with community problems is enhanced if ministers are sensitive to the intricate communication networks of rural communities. Community development practitioners find that drinking coffee with friends and neighbors at the local cafe can be a productive use of time. Ministers who reduce social distance between themselves and local people in similar ways probably are more effective and their tenures are more pleasant. Furthermore, as insiders, ministers can take positions on wider social and moral issues without the added critical attention given to outsiders.

References

Bedell, George C.; Leo Sandon, Jr.; Charles T. Wellborn
1975 *Religion in America* (New York: Macmillan)

Blizzard, Samuel W.
1956 "The Minister's Dilemma," *Christian Century* 73:508-9.

Brunner, Edmund de S.
1917 *The New Country Church Building* (New York: Mission Education Movement of the United States and Canada)

Earle, John R.; Dean D. Knudsen; Donald W. Shriver
1976 *Spindles and Spires: A Re-study of Religion and Social Change in Gastonia* (Atlanta: John Knox Press)

Glock, Charles Y., and Rodney Stark
1965 *Religion and Society in Tension* (Chicago: Rand McNally)

Hadden, Jeffrey K.
1969 *The Gathering Storm in the Churches* (Garden City, N.Y.: Doubleday & Co.)

Harrison, Paul M.
1959 *Authority and Power in the Free Church Tradition* (Princeton, N.J.: Princeton University Press)

Hepple, Lawrence M.
1958 *The Church in Rural Missouri: Part III, Clergymen in Rural Missouri.* Research Bulletin 633c (Columbia: Missouri Agricultural Experiment Station)

Hill, Samuel S., Jr.
1966 *Southern Churches in Crisis* (New York: Holt, Rinehart, & Winston)

Hunter, James D.
1983 *American Evangelicalism: Conservative Religion and the Quandary of Modernity* (New Brunswick, N.Y.: Rutgers University Press)

REFERENCES

Nelsen, Hart M., and Raymond H. Potvin
1977 "The Rural Church and Rural Religion: Analysis of Data from Children and Youth," *The Annals of Academy of Political and Social Science* 429:103-114.

Pauck, Wilhelm
1963 "Our Protestant Heritage," *Religion and Contemporary Society*, ed. Harold Stahmer (New York: Macmillan)

Pope, Liston
1942 *Millhands and Preachers* (New Haven, Conn.: Yale University Press)

Quinn, Bernard; Herman Anderson; Martin Bradley; Paul Goetting; Peggy Shriver
1982 *Churches and Church Membership in the United States, 1980* (Atlanta: Glenmary Research Center)

Roof, Wade Clark
1976 "Traditional Religion in Contemporary Society: A Theory of Local-Cosmopolitan Plausibility," *American Sociological Review* 41:195-208.

Schaller, Lyle E.
1982 *The Small Church Is Different* (Nashville: Abingdon Press)

Shoemaker, Floyd C.
1943 *Missouri and Missourians* (Chicago: Lewis Publishing Co.)

Sweet, William Warren
1950 *The Story of Religion in America*, 2nd rev. ed. (New York: Harper & Brothers)

Taylor, Carl C., and E. W. Lehmann
1920 *Ashland Community Survey*. Bulletin 173 (Columbia: Missouri Agricultural Experiment Station)

Troeltsch, Ernst
1960 *The Social Teaching of the Christian Churches*, trans. Olive Wyon. (New York: Harper & Row)

Vidich, Arthur J., and Joseph Bensman
1958 *Small Town in Mass Society: Class, Power and Religion in a Rural Community* (Princeton, N.J.: Princeton University Press)

Yates, Juanita
1987 "Parish at Hurricane Branch Continues Strong Tradition," *The Catholic Missourian*, June 26.

Appendix

Table 2.a*

FACILITIES BY MEMBERSHIP AND TYPE OF
CONGREGATION, 1952, 1967, 1982

Type of Facility	Percentage of Congregations Having Facility		
	1952	1967	1982
Kitchen Facilities			
Total	24.9	51.7	67.2
Mainline	32.7	60.4	74.0
Nonmainline	3.9	30.1	52.9
Under 50 Members	4.6	24.6	46.8
Mainline	4.7	22.3	49.4
Nonmainline	4.5	27.3	43.7
50-99 Members	16.1	45.7	64.0
Mainline	21.6	56.3	67.1
Nonmainline	2.0	22.9	58.3
100 Members or More	51.4	82.0	88.1
Mainline	53.3	85.2	92.3
Nonmainline	2.5	57.1	66.7
Dining Facilities			
Total	——	52.5	69.3
Mainline	——	61.0	73.6
Nonmainline	——	31.5	59.7
Under 50 Members	——	25.7	46.1
Mainline	——	25.5	48.2
Nonmainline	——	26.0	43.7
50–99 Members	——	48.3	69.1
Mainline	——	57.3	68.2
Nonmainline	——	29.2	70.8
100 Members or More	——	80.9	88.7
Mainline	——	83.9	90.3
Nonmainline	——	57.1	80.0

*Table numbers refer to chapter in which topic is discussed.

Table 2.a (continued)

Office for Minister

Total	11.6	23.0	41.8
Mainline	14.2	25.1	42.8
Nonmainline	3.9	17.8	39.5
Under 50 Members	2.0	5.8	22.1
Mainline	2.3	3.2	16.9
Nonmainline	1.5	9.1	28.2
50-99 Members	4.3	17.9	31.7
Mainline	5.4	15.5	26.1
Nonmainline	4.0	22.9	41.7
100 Members or More	26.0	43.2	66.7
Mainline	21.0	43.8	67.1
Nonmainline	25.0	38.1	63.3

Parsonage

Total	29.9	36.0	35.4
Mainline	33.8	39.6	40.7
Nonmainline	15.7	27.4	24.2
Under 50 Members	13.1	14.0	16.9
Mainline	1.9	6.4	10.8
Nonmainline	21.9	23.4	24.0
50–99 Members	19.3	23.8	24.1
Mainline	20.0	20.4	26.1
Nonmainline	15.7	31.2	20.4
100 Members or More	54.1	66.7	60.0
Mainline	55.9	71.0	65.8
Nonmainline	37.5	33.0	30.0

Piano

Total	——	88.1	90.3
Mainline	——	93.6	95.1
Nonmainline	——	74.6	79.9
Under 50 Members	——	85.4	88.3
Mainline	——	92.6	97.6
Nonmainline	——	76.6	77.5
50–99 Members		89.4	91.9
Mainline	——	98.1	98.9
Nonmainline	——	70.8	79.2
100 Members or More	——	89.6	90.8
Mainline	——	91.4	91.6
Nonmainline	——	76.2	86.7

Table 2.a (continued)

Organ

Total	——	28.9	46.8
Mainline	——	35.9	55.1
Nonmainline	——	11.6	28.9
Under 50 Members	——	7.6	22.7
Mainline	——	7.4	22.9
Nonmainline	——	7.8	22.5
50–99 Members	——	16.6	34.6
Mainline	——	19.4	38.6
Nonmainline	——	10.4	27.1
100 Members or More	——	59.0	76.1
Mainline	——	63.0	81.8
Nonmainline	——	28.6	46.7

Cemetery

Total	——	25.7	26.5
Mainline	——	27.9	31.0
Nonmainline	——	20.5	16.7
Under 50 Members	——	25.1	28.6
Mainline	——	26.6	39.8
Nonmainline	——	23.4	15.5
50–99 Members	——	26.5	25.6
Mainline	——	30.1	29.5
Nonmainline	——	18.8	18.4
100 Members or More	——	25.7	25.4
Mainline	——	27.2	27.1
Nonmainline	——	14.3	16.7

Table 3.a

PERCEPTION OF THE CONGREGATIONS'
MEMBERSHIP CHANGE
IN THE NEXT TEN YEARS

| Perception of Membership Change | Type of Congregation | | | |
| | Mainline | | Nonmainline | |
	No.	Percent	No.	Percent
All Churches				
Grow	175	54.7	111	77.6
Stay the Same	86	26.9	19	13.3
Decline	39	12.2	10	7.0
Close	20	6.2	3	2.1
Under 50 Members				
Grow	31	38.3	50	73.5
Stay the Same	17	21.0	8	11.8
Decline	18	22.2	7	10.3
Close	15	18.5	3	4.4
50–99 Members				
Grow	36	42.4	33	73.3
Stay the Same	32	37.6	9	20.0
Decline	13	15.3	3	6.7
Close	4	4.7	0	0.0
100 Members or More				
Grow	108	70.1	28	93.3
Stay the Same	37	24.0	2	6.7
Decline	8	5.2	0	0.0
Close	1	0.7	0	0.0

Table 3.b

GAINS AND LOSSES OF CONGREGATIONS BY POPULATION CHANGES OF TOWNSHIPS WHERE CONGREGATIONS ARE LOCATED

Population Change of Township	Gains and Losses of Congregations 1952–1982*						
	Number of Townships	Losses No.	Losses Percent	Gains No.	Gains Percent	Total Gains & Losses No.	Total Gains & Losses Percent
Increasing (Grew from 1950–1970 and from 1970–1980)	15	15	34.1	29	65.9	44	100
Decreasing (Lost from 1950–1970 and from 1970–1980)	37	51	80.9	12	19.1	63	100
Increasing/Decreasing (Grew from 1950–1970; lost from 1970–1980)	3	3	50.0	3	50.0	6	100
Decreasing/Increasing (Lost from 1950–1970; grew from 1970–1980)	44	61	53.0	54	47.0	115	100

Source: United States Census of Population: 1950, 1970, 1980
*Gains and losses were checked at two points: from 1952–1967 and from 1967–1982.

Table 4.a

RELIGIOUS SERVICES BY MEMBERSHIP AND
TYPE OF CONGREGATION, 1952, 1967, 1982

Type of Services	Percentage of Congregations Conducting Services		
	1952	1967	1982
Weekly Worship Services			
Total	45.4	70.3	86.0
Mainline	39.1	64.6	80.5
Nonmainline	62.7	84.2	97.5
Under 50 Members	37.0	54.4	74.0
Mainline	9.0	31.9	54.2
Nonmainline	71.2	81.8	97.2
50–99 Members	35.6	68.2	83.2
Mainline	29.5	61.2	76.1
Nonmainline	50.0	83.3	95.9
100 Members or More	61.8	86.9	97.8
Mainline	61.2	85.8	97.4
Nonmainline	75.0	95.2	100.0
Midweek Services			
Total	47.1	42.0	50.6
Mainline	37.7	33.7	38.9
Nonmainline	73.1	62.3	75.3
Under 50 Members	40.1	36.8	40.3
Mainline	16.9	16.0	18.1
Nonmainline	68.5	62.3	66.2
50–99 Members	47.2	39.1	50.4
Mainline	33.9	32.0	35.2
Nonmainline	76.5	54.2	77.6
100 Members or More	52.8	49.2	56.8
Mainline	51.2	45.1	51.0
Nonmainline	87.5	81.0	86.7

Table 4.a (continued)

Revivals

Total	65.9	64.4	57.9
Mainline	60.4	59.6	52.4
Nonmainline	81.3	76.0	69.6
Under 50 Members	59.3	53.8	49.7
Mainline	46.1	41.5	34.9
Nonmainline	75.3	68.8	67.1
50–99 Members	69.3	68.9	64.0
Mainline	61.6	64.1	56.8
Nonmainline	86.3	79.2	77.1
100 Members or More	68.5	70.5	65.8
Mainline	67.1	67.3	61.7
Nonmainline	100.0	95.2	86.7

Sunday Evening Services

Total	——	52.1	55.0
Mainline	——	42.3	43.3
Nonmainline	——	76.0	80.7
Under 50 Members	——	43.9	52.6
Mainline	——	21.3	30.1
Nonmainline	——	71.4	78.9
50–99 Members	——	53.6	54.0
Mainline	——	43.7	39.8
Nonmainline	——	75.0	79.6
100 Members or More	——	58.5	57.8
Mainline	——	53.7	52.3
Nonmainline	——	95.2	86.7

Table 4.b

SPECIFIC SUBORGANIZATIONS BY MEMBERSHIP AND
TYPE OF CONGREGATION, 1952, 1967, 1982

Type of Suborganization	Percentage of Congregations Having Suborganizations		
	1952	1967	1982
Sunday School			
Total	88.8	91.5	93.3
Mainline	87.9	92.2	94.3
Nonmainline	90.8	89.7	91.1
Under 50 Members	79.0	86.6	86.4
Mainline	73.0	87.2	85.5
Nonmainline	86.3	85.7	87.3
50–99 Members	95.7	96.0	96.3
Mainline	95.5	98.1	98.9
Nonmainline	96.0	91.7	91.7
100 Members or More	91.1	92.4	96.8
Mainline	90.6	91.4	96.8
Nonmainline	100.0	100.0	96.7
Women's Organization			
Total	56.5	56.2	52.3
Mainline	72.0	66.6	62.3
Nonmainline	20.5	30.8	31.2
Under 50 Members	30.9	31.0	29.2
Mainline	43.8	37.2	34.9
Nonmainline	15.1	23.4	22.5
50–99 Members	54.9	50.3	47.1
Mainline	70.3	60.2	53.4
Nonmainline	21.6	29.2	35.4
100 Members or More	86.6	84.7	78.4
Mainline	87.7	87.7	83.2
Nonmainline	62.5	61.9	53.3

Table 4.b (continued)

Type of Suborganization	Percentage of Congregations Having Suborganizations		
	1952	1967	1982
Youth Organization			
Total	37.6	39.4	38.3
Mainline	44.2	43.2	39.2
Nonmainline	18.9	30.1	36.3
Under 50 Members	16.7	14.6	19.5
Mainline	15.7	7.4	13.3
Nonmainline	17.8	23.4	26.8
50–99 Members	30.2	33.1	25.7
Mainline	36.9	35.0	19.3
Nonmainline	15.7	29.2	37.5
100 Members or More	63.1	67.8	65.4
Mainline	63.7	69.1	65.2
Nonmainline	50.0	57.1	66.7
Study Group*			
Total	——	——	42.3
Mainline	——	——	45.2
Nonmainline	——	——	35.8
Under 50 Members	——	——	26.6
Mainline	——	——	21.7
Nonmainline	——	——	32.4
50–99 Members	——	——	41.2
Mainline	——	——	44.3
Nonmainline	——	——	35.4
100 Members or More	——	——	56.3
Mainline	——	——	58.4
Nonmainline	——	——	44.8

Table 4.b (continued)

Type of Suborganization	Percentage of Congregations Having Suborganizations		
	1952	1967	1982
Choir			
Total	35.6	40.7	43.6
Mainline	42.9	33.7	50.6
Nonmainline	15.2	16.4	28.7
Under 50 Members	14.0	13.5	19.5
Mainline	18.0	16.0	20.5
Nonmainline	12.3	10.4	18.3
50–99 Members	27.2	25.8	33.8
Mainline	33.3	29.1	38.6
Nonmainline	13.7	18.8	25.0
100 Members or More	61.5	59.0	73.0
Mainline	62.0	62.3	74.2
Nonmainline	50.0	33.3	66.7
Men's Organization			
Total	12.9	15.8	17.5
Mainline	17.0	21.2	21.9
Nonmainline	1.5	2.7	8.3
Under 50 Members	0.6	5.3	5.2
Mainline	1.1	8.5	6.0
Nonmainline	0.0	1.3	4.2
50–99 Members	7.4	4.0	8.1
Mainline	9.9	4.9	5.7
Nonmainline	2.0	2.1	12.5
100 Members or More	29.0	35.5	35.7
Mainline	29.8	38.9	40.0
Nonmainline	12.5	9.5	13.3

Table 4.b (continued)

| Type of Suborganization | Percentage of Congregations Having Suborganizations | | |
	1952	1967	1982
Young-Adults' Organization			
Total	8.0	7.0	9.2
Mainline	10.0	8.6	10.5
Nonmainline	2.3	4.1	6.4
Under 50 Members	1.9	2.9	4.6
Mainline	3.4	1.1	6.0
Nonmainline	0.0	5.2	2.8
50–99 Members	4.9	4.6	4.4
Mainline	4.5	6.8	4.6
Nonmainline	5.9	0.0	4.2
100 Members or More	16.2	13.7	17.3
Mainline	17.0	14.2	16.8
Nonmainline	0.0	9.5	20.0
Older-Adults' Organization			
Total	2.6	5.0	4.7
Mainline	3.5	5.9	5.4
Nonmainline	0.0	2.7	3.2
Under 50 Members	0.0	1.2	0.7
Mainline	0.0	1.1	0.0
Nonmainline	0.0	1.3	1.4
50–99 Members	0.6	4.0	1.5
Mainline	0.9	3.9	2.3
Nonmainline	0.0	4.2	0.0
100 Members or More	6.7	9.3	10.8
Mainline	7.0	5.9	10.3
Nonmainline	0.0	2.7	13.3

*data for study group not available for 1952 and 1967

Table 4.c

EDUCATIONAL PROGRAMS BY MEMBERSHIP AND TYPE OF CONGREGATION, 1952, 1967, 1982

Type of Educational Programs	Percentage of Congregations Having Programs		
	1952	1967	1982
Daily Vacation Bible School			
Total	45.7	52.1	50.8
Mainline	57.7	60.4	59.3
Nonmainline	12.7	31.5	32.9
Under 50 Members	20.4	22.2	19.5
Mainline	24.7	23.4	21.7
Nonmainline	15.1	20.8	16.9
50–99 Members	43.6	55.0	47.1
Mainline	58.9	63.1	50.0
Nonmainline	9.8	37.5	41.7
100 Members or More	71.3	77.6	81.0
Mainline	74.1	80.2	84.4
Nonmainline	12.5	57.1	63.3
Religious and Educational Films			
Total	36.8	46.7	54.1
Mainline	45.0	53.5	56.8
Nonmainline	14.2	30.1	48.4
Under 50 Members	16.1	21.1	29.2
Mainline	19.1	19.1	26.5
Nonmainline	12.3	23.4	32.4
50–99 Members	37.4	36.4	55.2
Mainline	47.3	55.3	50.0
Nonmainline	15.7	27.1	64.6
100 Members or More	55.6	71.0	73.9
Mainline	57.1	72.2	76.6
Nonmainline	25.0	61.9	60.0

Table 4.c (continued)

Training for New Members*			
Total	70.6	35.2	40.6
Mainline	73.0	41.5	47.7
Nonmainline	64.2	19.9	25.5
Under 50 Members	59.3	12.9	17.5
Mainline	57.3	13.8	21.7
Nonmainline	61.6	11.7	12.7
50–99 Members	71.0	25.3	37.5
Mainline	73.0	32.0	38.6
Nonmainline	66.7	25.0	35.4
100 Members or More	80.9	60.7	64.7
Mainline	81.2	63.6	68.8
Nonmainline	75.0	38.1	43.3

*Each of the three surveys asked whether religious training was offered to new members. Positive responses for 1967 and 1982 were similar—35 percent and 41 percent of the congregations respectively. However, the report of training for new members was higher in 1952—71 percent of the congregations. This difference seems large, considering the modest differences in other activities. The questions on the questionnaires were the same, but it was noted that in the report of the 1952 survey, that training was almost always done by the minister, while in the later surveys it was considered more a program of the church. It seems likely that the question was interpreted differently in 1952 than in 1967 and 1982. In 1952, there appeared to be few differences on the basis of size or type of congregation in the proportion of congregations offering training to new members. However, in both 1967 and 1982, larger congregations were more likely than smaller congregations, and mainline congregations more likely than nonmainline congregations to provide that training.

Table 6.a

WORK SITUATIONS OF MINISTERS IN RURAL MISSOURI BY TYPE OF CONGREGATION, 1952, 1967, 1982

Ministers' Work Situation	1952 Percent	1967 Percent	1982 Percent
Serve Only One Congregation			
Total	47.3	63.3	74.2
Mainline	38.1	54.4	66.0
Nonmainline	75.3	78.2	92.5
Tenure in Present Location			
Total			
Less than 2 Years	44.1	45.5	27.9
2–3.9 Years	29.3	27.7	29.1
4 Years or More	26.7	26.7	43.0
Mainline			
Less than 2 Years	43.4	44.2	30.0
2–3.9 Years	30.9	30.4	27.8
4 Years or More	25.8	25.4	42.2
Nonmainline			
Less than 2 Years	45.8	47.9	23.0
2–3.9 Years	25.3	23.2	32.0
4 Years or More	28.9	28.9	45.0
Have a Secular Occupation			
Total	58.3	48.1	44.9
Mainline	52.3	38.7	42.1
Nonmainline	76.5	64.1	50.9

Table 6.b

MINISTERS' PREFERENCES IN TIME SPENT ON 12 ACTIVITIES

Activity	Time Preferred (Percent of Ministers)		
	More	Less	Same
Sermon Preparation	56.8	0.9	42.3
Private Meditation and Study	68.8	0.6	30.7
Conduct Worship Services	25.3	1.8	72.9
Visiting Sick Members	40.5	7.7	51.8
Calling on Prospective Members	71.1	0.9	28.0
Other Pastoral Calling	47.6	2.1	50.3
Counseling of Members with Special Problems	50.0	5.1	44.9
Administrative Work	21.1	25.9	53.0
Attendance at Church Committee Meetings	17.9	16.1	66.0
Attendance at Denominational Meetings	22.8	9.6	67.6
Attendance at Interdenominational Meetings	24.3	4.2	71.6
Attendance at Civic Club Meetings and Community Programs	29.2	5.7	65.2

Table 7.a

RESPONSES OF MINISTERS TO SELECTED SOCIAL AND MORAL ISSUES BY THEOLOGICAL POSITION

Position on Issues	Liberal No.	Percent	Conservative No.	Percent	Fundamentalist No.	Percent
Social Issues						
Federal Aid to Private Schools						
Support	10	20.4	28	15.9	15	13.6
Oppose	28	57.1	123	69.9	67	60.9
Neutral	11	22.5	25	14.2	28	25.5
Capital Punishment						
Support	12	24.5	116	65.9	80	72.7
Oppose	28	57.1	40	22.7	14	12.7
Neutral	9	18.4	20	11.4	16	14.6
Racial Integration						
Support	42	85.7	149	84.7	76	69.1
Oppose	0	——	12	6.8	11	10.0
Neutral	7	14.3	15	8.5	23	20.9
Workfare						
Support	27	55.1	139	79.0	87	79.1
Oppose	12	24.5	15	8.5	8	7.3
Neutral	10	20.4	22	12.5	15	13.6
Limitations on Nuclear Arms						
Support	41	83.7	101	57.4	56	50.5
Oppose	2	4.1	24	13.6	19	17.1
Neutral	6	12.2	51	29.0	36	32.4
ERA (Equal Rights Amendment)						
Support	29	59.2	30	17.0	6	5.5
Oppose	15	30.6	111	63.1	89	80.9
Neutral	5	10.2	35	19.9	15	13.6
Right to Choose Abortion						
Support	28	57.1	23	13.1	7	6.4
Oppose	15	30.6	133	75.6	99	90.0
Neutral	6	12.2	20	11.4	4	3.6

Table 7.a (continued)

RESPONSES OF MINISTERS TO SELECTED SOCIAL AND MORAL ISSUES BY THEOLOGICAL POSITION

Position on Issues	*Liberal* No.	*Percent*	*Conservative* No.	*Percent*	*Fundamentalist* No.	*Percent*

Moral Issues

Sale of Alcoholic Beverages						
Support	12	24.5	23	13.1	5	4.6
Oppose	18	36.7	123	69.9	100	90.9
Neutral	19	38.8	30	17.0	5	4.6
Smoking						
Support	6	12.2	12	6.8	1	0.9
Oppose	24	49.0	126	71.6	93	84.6
Neutral	19	38.8	38	21.6	16	14.6
Social Dancing						
Support	25	51.0	40	22.7	6	5.5
Oppose	8	16.3	71	40.3	90	81.8
Neutral	16	32.7	65	36.9	14	12.7
Mixed Swimming (of the Sexes)						
Support	29	59.2	85	48.3	34	30.6
Oppose	5	10.2	27	15.3	43	38.7
Neutral	15	30.6	64	36.4	33	29.7
Social Drinking						
Support	14	28.6	18	10.2	2	1.8
Oppose	17	34.7	134	76.1	103	93.6
Neutral	18	36.7	24	13.6	5	4.6
Voluntary Prayer in Schools						
Support	26	53.1	114	64.8	88	80.0
Oppose	18	36.7	37	21.0	12	10.9
Neutral	5	10.2	25	14.2	10	9.1